ANNIE'S W
By Mackenzie Brown
Copyright 2014 Mackenzie Brown
Mack Brown Books (c).

Paul,
'A man among Men'
Dave/Mack

With love, fond memories and great respect for my
Grandparents Anne and Angus

"Never in the field of human conflict was so much owed by so many to so few."
- Winston Churchill

Also by the same author

The Shifting
The Book of Souls
Lost Boys (The Black Knight Series #1)
Prince of the City – The Cat's Whiskers
Prince of the City – Nine Lives

Fanny's story

1

Archduke Ferdinand was murdered on the 28th of June 1914.

This was only five days before Mam died and I recall sneaking a look at my husband's *Echo* shortly after the shooting. The story argued that because of Ferdinand's death, life would never be the same again for any of us and the repercussions would be great and far-reaching. I doubt whether the author realised at the time how prophetic his words were to become.

And I remember thinking this was also true for each and every one of her children, the day Frances Newland died.

Mam was Fanny Wilson when she married our Father John Newland during September of 1889. They must have looked a proper mis-matched couple, she so slender and petite, not to mention pretty as a picture. Her big brown eyes were the first thing anybody noticed when a person first met our Mam. In stark contrast my Father was a great gangly, lolloping giant of a thing, according to the woman he eventually married that is. As the years passed by and many a pint of beer spilled down his throat, my Father filled out and became quite an imposing figure, but there was never any doubt that Mam was in charge. She had a kind of Svengali hold over him and I honestly believe if she had asked him to jump into the Mersey fully clothed, with a weight tied to his ankles, he'd have done it. He absolutely doted on her every word. In fact I've never witnessed another person love somebody, or something so much.

Mam was mostly easy to love, but her temper was quick and vicious. I remember one time when my brother John dropped and smashed a teapot that had been passed down to Mam from my Grandmother. Mother was cutting up some bread at the time and perhaps to steady himself John placed his left hand on the breadboard, looking down at the broken, steaming mess at his feet. Mam's big eyes darkened and as God's my witness, she chopped down at his hand with the bread knife. If he hadn't made a fist on the board without realising the danger he was in, he'd have lost most of his fingers. Mam was horrified when she came 'round and in her defence she usually came to her senses as quickly as the black temper took hold of her. So as a rule of thumb, it was a good idea to clear out of her way until she'd calmed down, as she was liable to do just about anything.

There was poverty and disease on the streets of Liverpool in those days and it was no surprise considering the lack of general hygiene there was back then, with so many families crammed together in row upon row of tiny houses. But I can only talk about us and the way we lived was all I knew and when I look back on my childhood it was mostly a happy one.

Father worked as a Journeyman - plasterer, which meant one week he could be working around the corner and the next miles from our house. Before I was married, I remember he often came home when we were all in bed, but he always brought home every penny he'd earned and handed it over to Mam, who kept a very tight rein on the family purse strings. I can't ever remember going without food. There was always bread and potatoes to eat and the luxury of meat at least once a week. Father like most working class men of his era liked a drink and Mam allowed him to exercise his vice each and every Friday night, but she was cunning enough to want him out of the way on bath night. This was the night Mam would light a roaring fire and get John to drag the old tin bath in from the yard. Then she'd proceed to fill the bath with hot water from the stove, a painstaking and relatively dangerous operation. We all knew of course that it wasn't a good idea for Mam to lose her temper with a scalding hot pan in her hand; for that reason we were always on our best behaviour on bath night.

When we lived at home John and I were roped in to help. She liked to bath the little ones first. That was her system; the youngest got the cleanest water. In fact by the time John and I took our turns the water was a filthy grey colour, but Mam always had a hot pan or two ready, to at least make sure it was warm.

Then we'd all snuggle up together in our tiny bedroom. The girls; Minnie, Lillian and myself in one bed. The boys; John, William, Robert, James and Lawrence, top to tail in another. And we were a happy bunch, gabbing and larking around, but John and I would eventually shush the others, until one by one we drifted off to sleep. We were particularly happy every Friday because not only were our bellies full, but also we were cleaner than we'd been for days.

2

Our happiness and wellbeing was all down to Mam. She was the family heartbeat, the driving force. She organised and fed our small army of Newlands. There was no time for molly coddling the little ones, life was hard and tough love was often the order of the day and if anyone got out of hand, she could always threaten our silent, brooding Father.

When she fell pregnant with our unborn sister, John and I saw to it that between us we gradually did a little more as she grew bigger, even though we were both married and running our own homes by this time.

Hindsight is a wonderful thing, but the more I think back about her final pregnancy, the warning signs were there. Mam was generally happy and healthy when she was carrying each of the little ones, but that last time she was pale and uncomfortable in the early days. She didn't complain mind, perhaps she put her problems down to age, but later on her face was red as a turkey-cock's and it seemed to change shape from its usual small and pert and take on a moon like shape.

I'm sure it bothered her, but if she'd wanted to seek medical advice, where would she have gone? This was before the days of the National Health Service, that didn't come into effect until 1948. In those days only the privileged could afford the services of a Doctor, unless by some miracle the said Doctor was a friend or relative. Instead people like us relied on a neighbour to assist with the birth of children and the laying out of the dead. Every street had one such person and in our case this was Mrs Maguire, a coarse brunette, with a thick Southern Irish accent. In return for services rendered, neighbours would pay her whatever they could afford, some gave coal, others food, including pies and cakes from baking day, others saw that her husband never had to pay for a drink. In return Mrs Maguire was present at every birth in the street including my own and was called upon after every death.

On the morning of the 2nd July 1914, I'd arranged to sleep over at Mam's to give her a hand. I remember hearing Father leaving to go to work and the sound of boots and clogs on the cobbled streets, as the working men of Liverpool started their day.

I must have dozed off again as I was awakened by the cries of pain from Mam's room. It took me a while to come round, but the butterflies in my stomach told me something was terribly wrong and I shook myself awake and rushed to her side. What I found was my red-faced Mother writhing in agony, sweat pouring from her brow.

Her blood shot eyes turned on me momentarily and God help her she smiled, seeing my worried face and said,

"Don't worry Fanny, it's my time that's all. Run and get Mrs Maguire she'll know what to do. Give the little ones a bit of breakfast and see they get off to school."

"I heard you cry out in pain," I said.

"Look I'll be fine as long as you do as I ask love."

I only wish that had been true.

My eldest brother John who was very close to Mam, was also worried about her and turned up unexpectedly. With his help I fed the young ones and walked them to school. Reaching the school gates, something about Mam's condition worried me, call it intuition or an inner voice, but whatever it was something urged me to hurry back. John who should have headed straight to work from the school gates, came with me and I wasn't able to persuade him from doing otherwise.

When we reached Harrogate Street, there were unmerciful screams coming from Mam's door and I left John wringing his hands and pacing in front of the cold fireplace, as I rushed upstairs.

Mrs Maguire looked troubled. Mam was in some distress, oblivious to my presence.

"Oh tank d'Lord you came back girl. I've tried everything I know but I can't stop the bleeding. Be a good girl and run and get Doc Parsons as quickly as you can," she told me, looking almost as worried as John.

I didn't need telling twice. I sent John to alert Father who was working locally that day and I rushed into the street at full pelt, determined to return with a Doctor we couldn't possibly afford.

Doctor Parsons was fresh out of medical school and new to the district and it was rumoured he charged reasonable rates. He didn't look much older than me. A slight man with a thin, pale face, but I saw compassion in his eyes and it gave me hope. He came easily enough after one look at my face, setting off at such a pace, I was forced to run to stay ahead of him, but I wasn't complaining.

I prayed to any God who might be listening that I'd brought him in time.

I took up John's earlier position downstairs as Doctor Parsons rushed to our Mother's side. Minutes later the cries from my baby sister filled me with optimism and I remember smiling at the first sounds of new life, believing all was not lost, but my happiness was blighted almost immediately, as Father burst into the house, his heavy footsteps thudding on the stairs. I followed the noise and took up a position at the bottom of the narrow staircase, standing beside an equally dumbstruck John, as a rather forlorn looking Doctor Parsons appeared on the top step.

Father stopped dead, his gargantuan frame casting a shadow over the Doctor's sweating face.

"Well?" was all he asked.

"You have a fine, healthy daughter Mr Newland."

"I don't care about tha', 'ow's my wife? 'Ow is Fanny for Christ's sake?"

"I'm so sorry Mr Newland, there was nothing I could do. She'd just lost too much blood."

"No!" He roared, as hot tears burned my cheeks. I was sure he was going to strike the Doctor. Instead he merely took hold of the man's arm and pulled the stunned Doctor out of the way, sending him down the stairs head first. Fortunately he was able to put an arm out to steady himself and as he descended, he glanced back, as if to make sure my Father had gone.

"I'm so sorry," he added before passing John and I and making his way out into the warm sunshine.

Father sounded like a wounded animal, sobbing and wailing and the commotion must have disturbed Mrs Maguire, who made her way down the stairs carrying a pink bundle.

"Just give your Father a minute and then you can pay your respects if you're both up to it."

I remember nodding, but there was no sound from John. I'm not sure how much time passed, but we were all seated in the front room when Father's heavier than usual footsteps signalled his descent. Mrs Maguire stood, still holding the baby and moved to where she knew Father would be.

"I'm so very sorry John," I heard her say.

Father merely grunted and said something incomprehensible.

"D'ya want to take a look at the little one now, ar' she's a bonny little 'ting."

"I want none of it!"

"But what about the children? The little one?"

"Didn't you 'ear me woman? I said I wanted none of it. The only thing I ever loved on God's earth lies dead up those stairs. I want none of it without my Fanny!"

And his words were so loud, they'd have heard him in the next street. He looked back at John and I through tear stained eyes, before turning on his heel without so much as a word to either of us.

I never laid eyes on my Father again.

3

    We were abandoned and I feared it would be the poorhouse for my younger brothers and sisters and the thought of them spending one night in such a place filled me with dread. Stories about conditions and goings on at such places filtered through to us and although I felt some of what we'd heard might be exaggerated, I was in no doubt, despair and disease was a way of life for the poor souls who were trapped there.

    John and I were in no position to take them all in and if we took one or two, how would we choose?

    Little did I know that thanks to Mrs Maguire, the neighbours had already put their heads together and a plan of action had been put in place, together with the unofficial agreement of our local Police Constable. It was possible to make such arrangements in those days, when common sense often was the order of the day.

    Days and weeks passed and John and I fed and looked after our siblings with help from the kindness of the people from Harrogate Street. Anne was placed in the care of a barren couple who lived opposite us. Mr and Mrs Groves were decent law abiding people. They already had a two-year-old stepson, Tommy; who had been acquired without the need to go through the appropriate adoption channels of the day.

    Despite the Groves taking little Anne off our hands, my naiveté led me to believe our Father would eventually come to his senses.

    But nothing of the sort happened.

    Without my knowledge, letters had been despatched to members of the Newland clan by the authorities, including those who lived on the other side of the Mersey, which in those days was a fair distance to travel.

    In the days that passed, relatives I'd never laid eyes on, would show up and take our brothers and sisters away from us in ones and twos. Lawrence who was only three was whisked away across the Mersey, as were Lillian who was four and James and Robert who were seven and nine respectively. Minnie who was a sullen ten years of age came to live with me and William who was thirteen moved in with John and his wife. It seemed the decision about who we took had been made for us.

    It was heartbreaking and I secretly knew that despite all the tears and promises to the little ones, it was unlikely we'd all stay in touch. Mam's demise had been the death of our happy little family and when her heart stopped beating, it had been the death knell for the Newlands of Harrogate Street. The tears and bewilderment on the faces of the little ones, who were beyond understanding was all too much for me and I was inconsolable. I grieved for my Mother and everything that had died with her.

Anne was the only one of us to remain in Harrogate Street.

My own home was only a few streets away and I made a vow in the presence of God, that I'd retain contact with my baby sister, the last of Mam's children.

The day I deposited her in the arms of Mrs Groves, I swear I could see my Mother's face. Later that evening when I was alone with my thoughts, I felt deeply sad for the innocent babe, who had no choice in her fate, but who was forced to begin her journey in this world without a family. This on top of everything else sent the waterworks spilling down my face for my baby sister, little orphan Annie.

Anne's Mother, Frances Newland

Anne's Story - part 1

1

I was never a scholar. Yet I wonder how much of it I might have enjoyed if the teachers hadn't ruled the place with an iron rod. It was nothing for them to rap an unsuspecting child on the knuckles with a wooden ruler for no more than a lapse of concentration. The cane was another favourite weapon and the blackboard duster too, could be quite a weapon, when launched across the classroom with full force. This was like a red rag to a bull to me and I decided quickly I wouldn't stand for it.

I freely admit I struggled to maintain my concentration in a place that bore no resemblance to real life for me, when there was always something better I could be doing.

For this reason I played truant as often as I could.

My stepbrother Tommy, knew what I was up to and even though he was a couple of years older than me, I threatened to flatten him or put eggshell in his sandwiches if he told on me. We'd go into school together and take the register, but at the first chance, which was usually the morning break, I'd be over the railings and back into our cosy home in no time at all. Old Groves was away at work and his wife Eleanor, the lazy old cow; was six feet under by then. She'd died from consumption when I was nine.

So I had the place to myself and it might well have been my own.

From the day I could walk Mrs Eleanor Groves made it her business to teach me everything there was about keeping a house, from black leading the grate, to cleaning out the toilet bowl in the outside lavatory. You'd think she was schooling me in the art of housewifery, to prepare me for the life I would live if I was ever lucky enough to take a husband. But no, the crafty mare was in the business of making her own life easier. Once I could do it all, including the cooking, she started to develop what she referred to as 'her spells.' She could have as many as four or five in a day and the funny thing was, she seemed to become light headed whenever a brush, mop or duster was in her hand, not to mention a serving spoon.

Don't misunderstand me, she taught me a great deal about housework, darning and cooking and let's face it was what a woman was supposed to know in those days. It got so that on baking day the neighbours'd be commenting on the delicious smells coming from our house and I was warned to keep my mouth shut, when she'd pass my apple and rhubarb pies off as her own. If her motives had been different, perhaps I'd have a kind word to say about her. I admit I shed a tear when she passed on, but it was for Groves sake really. He loved her and she could do no wrong in his eyes. But I was glad I no longer had her looking over my shoulder all the time.

Old Groves wasn't a talker; he'd say it all with his expressions. I knew for example he missed her terribly and for him alone I wish she was still around. He seemed to walk about with a great weight on his shoulders for years after her death and most things that once came easy to him, were quite an effort for a long time after her death.

I can read his face like a book and can always tell when I've let him down. There's never any punishment, just a kind of hurt look, but it's enough to knot up my insides. Take the time I was first caught playing truant. After six of the best on my small hand I was marched home and when Groves walked in, no doubt weary and hungry from a hard day's graft, he was greeted by the condescending tone of the teacher. I'd have been happier if he'd simply tanned my hide, but all I got was a look of total disappointment and a shake of the head. This was followed by the silent treatment for a day or so, which in truth was not a lot different from his usual word or two. He was quite a one old Groves. Why use two words when a nod or the shake of the head would do. I loved him though and I can honestly say that. He never once raised his hand to me, which is more than I could say for her, whose adage was why give one clout, when ten will get the job done. But as I was saying, Groves was good to me, he understood me and there aren't many men who can put a claim to that one.

2

William Groves was a blacksmith, like his Father before him. He worked at the tram terminal in Birkenhead, which was on the opposite banks of the Mersey to Liverpool. It was and still is referred to as the one eyed City by some locals, for nothing more mysterious than the fact the spelling of the place contains a solitary letter 'I'. That says more about the sense of humour of the average Merseysider than anything else.

Birkenhead from Walton on the Hill is still a bit of journey to work even now, but this was a trip and a half in the early 1920's. It would involve walking to the tram station, taking the tram to the Pier Head, where he'd catch a ferry across the Mersey, that was grey and polluted in those days, by the heavy industry that lived off the rich pickings of the port of Liverpool.

He was fortunate enough though, to enjoy employment during the golden age of the tram on Merseyside. Trams were his life and Old Groves had very few outside interests. When he was in the mood he'd recite the history of the tram to me and I'm surprised how much of it stuck, considering my usual reaction to learning of any kind. I was happy to see him with a glass of stout ale in his hand, in full flow. He wasn't what you'd call a drinker or a talker, but once he was under the influence of his favourite subject, there was no stopping him. He'd tell me how American, George Francis Train introduced horse drawn trams to both London and Birkenhead in 1861 and although they weren't an immediate success, they eventually caught on, particularly in Birkenhead, even though the London trams' stopped running after only six months service. That's how come Birkenhead lays claim to have run the first ever trams in Europe, something Groves was very proud of. It was the poor roads of the time that helped the trams Old Groves'd say. Two horses could pull 50 passengers very cheaply on those smooth rails and that's a darn sight more than any horse drawn carriage could manage.

His job was to shoe horses and work at mending damaged rails, but when the rails were electrified in 1901 he told me that much of the romance was gone for him. He'd work all day bending hot metal, so it was no surprise that through Monday to Saturday, he'd hardly have a word to say to us. The work was carried out in extreme heat and was back breaking.

Tommy and I took turns reading the paper to him after meal times and I'd do anything to miss my turn. I didn't mind reading titbits for myself, but Groves had never learned to read and insisted that every word from local evening paper, the *Liverpool Echo* was read to him. Tommy'd often volunteer to take my turn in if I agreed to clean Groves boots for him, or even Tommy's football boots, that were always caked in mud. I'd even take his turn doing the dishes, that's how desperate I was to escape this chore; but if there was a game of football, or rounders going on in the street, I was out of luck.

Tommy was a typical lad and loved playing sports above everything else.

By 1926 I was 12 years old. My world was truancy, housework, cooking and avoiding reading the evening paper to my beloved stepFather.

Quite a girl you might say.

I was prone to sudden and severe bouts of anger and depression and little did I realise at the time that although some of this was because of my personality, a good deal of my problems related to an incident in 1921. Something I'll carry with me all of my days.

3

I was a happy and healthy seven-year old.

My eldest sister Fanny and even older brother John had been regular visitors' at least once a month and tended to call on us after church on Sundays. I have to admit that although I was glad to see Fanny in particular, the preparation for their visit was always a cause of consternation for me. I'd usually bake something and be forced by Groves silent mouth but watchful eye, to be on my best behaviour.

"Best foot forward," he'd often say to me on the morning of their visit. The only other comment he ever made, was how much Fanny and I were alike,

"You're like two peas in a pod," he'd often say.

And I took this in the spirit it was intended, after all Mrs Groves was always saying how much my sister resembled my natural Mother and as she was a source of never ending curiosity on my part, I was happy to be connected with her in any way whatsoever. If Fanny was the image of my natural Mother and we were supposedly so much alike, the chances were I too favoured my natural Mother in looks. As an innocent seven-year old, this delighted me.

But that Sunday was different. My brother who was always a silent, brooding visitor, made old Groves seem like the most talkative man in Liverpool. He was incapable of little more than grunting in my direction, whenever he came with Fanny on one of her visits.

But that particular Sunday he turned up alone.

His dress seemed smarter than usual, but his complexion as always, pale and pasty. And instead of calling at the house, he approached Groves, with Tommy and I in his wake, as we were leaving church.

I was in my Sunday best and Groves I believe knew more than he was letting on. John seemed nervous and as he shook Groves's heavily callused hand and asked if I could accompany him, paying his respects to an uncle of ours who recently had passed away. I turned to look up at Groves impassive face praying he'd say no, but he simply said,

"It's only right and proper that she does lad."

If looks could kill, he'd have died on the spot.

My hands were covered in white lace gloves, I'd been told were once my Mother's, and were far too big for me. John took hold of my left hand and literally yanked me away from Groves and my worried looking stepbrother, almost taking the loose fitting glove only.

He said nothing at all as we reached the main road and passed street after street of terraced housing, each one looked exactly the same to me. I must explain that in those days, corner shops, pubs and funeral directors stood at the top of almost every street and it was at one of the latter we stopped.

In my disturbed state the name of the establishment was a blur and as I was drawn inside a dark, musty smelling place, we were met by a grey, thin-faced man in dark clothing. To my seven-year-old nostrils he smelled funny, along with the place itself, that smelled none too sweet. John and I followed him into the bowels of the place, the experience taking on a dreamlike quality for me.

He presented us with a series of cubicles, separated by chocolate brown curtains and stood for a moment before theatrically drawing back the curtain to the fourth cubicle to our right. Inside on a metal stand was a coffin and inside the body of an enormous man. Although John was still holding my hand I instinctively backed away, but he held me firm.

I'd never before laid eyes on a dead body.

I wanted to turn and run.

The mountain of a man laid out before me looked like a marble statue, set in an unnatural pose by the funeral director. On his eyes rested two pennies and I tried to focus on them, rather than the man's pallid face. He meant nothing to me, but my close proximity to death was enough to make me want to retch.

I turned to look at John for a reaction and realised he was sobbing. I stupidly assumed he'd been close to the dead man and patted his arm trying my seven-year old best to comfort him.

"Y'know who this is don't you Anne?" he said, taking deep breaths to try to control his sobbing.

"Ar' Uncle?"

"This is Joseph Newland Anne, ar' Father."

"No it can't be, 'e's been dead for ages, 'e died before I was born, this can't be 'im. 'Ow could 'e live around 'ere and not wanna' see me?"

"Anne 'e was....."

"......'E was what? Say what y'like, but nothing makes it right."

Suddenly the unfamiliar smells and the claustrophobic atmosphere of the place, coupled with the news that had tumbled from my brother's lips, sent my head into a spin and before I knew it I was running for the exit. Once out in the sunshine again, I was comforted by the feel of the wind on my skin and was relieved to breathing in fresh air again. I turned the corner into an unknown street and dropped to the floor, my back to the warm brickwork. My own tears now falling onto gloved hands, covering my face.

I don't know how much time passed, but John eventually appeared and stood over me.

"Come on Anne, we need to talk."

I don't remember answering, just climbing to my feet and trudging after him. We walked to a small area of recreational ground at the bottom of Heyworth Street and the junction of Rupert Lane and neither of us said a word, until we found an empty bench and both dropped onto it. The small grassed area was filled with children playing in their Sunday best and Mothers and Fathers dressed in the same fashion, enjoying the rare sunshine and respite from the Monday to Saturday grind. There were smiles and laughter all about me, when my insides were churning. Was I cursed? I'd heard about such things, people born under a dark star, others that lived under the Indian sign. My head was spinning and my breakfast wanted to escape from my body, but even as I felt pins and needles in my hands and a film of sweat covered my body, I refused to give in. Even though I was very young, I found the strength from somewhere to pull myself together, in what would prove to be one of the defining moments of my life.

John had been talking, but for how long I couldn't know.

"It wasn't just you Anne, 'e didn't want anything to do with any of us. When mam died, she took most of what was good in 'im with 'er."

He'd been looking down at the ground, but forgetting his shyness for a moment, he lifted his head and his red rimmed eyes looked into mine.

"At least that's whar' I tell myself."

For the first time I felt something for my silent, brooding brother and perhaps understood why he was this way, but I was far too young to put any of this into words.

"Did you know thar' I worked with 'im on the same buildin' site a couple a times? But whenever 'e looked my way, it was as if 'e didn't know me. Not once did 'e acknowledge thar' 'e knew me. Imagine 'ow that felt?"

"I'm sorry for you John, but what I don't get, is why you or Fanny didn't tell me 'e was alive? Why lie to me?"

He put his face in his cupped hands and ruffled his short mousy hair.

"Oh I can't answer thar' Anne. We only did what we thought best at the time. To be 'onest, Fanny didn't want me to bring you today. She'll go spare if she knows I told you all a this."

I don't know why, but his bravery appealed to something in me and the tension seemed to offer some form of release and before I realised, hot tears were rolling down my cheeks again and I heard myself say, "I'm glad you told me John. Thank you."

4

In the years that followed Tommy, old Groves and I grew closer than ever. We were like three pieces of cloth on the same garment. But despite our biological differences, we worked to keep our dysfunctional family together and we were happy in our own way.

How they coped with my mood swings I'll never know, but they did it somehow.

So often wrapped up in my own self-pity, I regularly forgot that Tommy had been orphaned just like me, yet he got on with life without complaint and without the comfort of contact from any of his relatives. His Mother and Father were both dead, or so he'd been told and like me I'm sure he often wondered what life might have been like in the bosom of his own flesh and blood, yet he never brought the subject up. He was Mr happy go lucky. He had a round cheeky face, he was quick witted and an exceptional sportsman. In addition to having the desire that most men have for playing sports, Tommy had boundless energy and fabulous hand to eye co-ordination, a requirement if you want to play sports at the highest level.

As a young man he was the best at every school or street sport, you could name; rounders, football, cricket, sprinting, the list went on. He even went on to play the fledgling sport of baseball and football at the highest level.

Thankfully he was the opposite of me in temperament and I can't ever remember him losing his temper once, which is a damn sight more than can be said for me. I recall throwing a scrubbing brush at him and bloodying his nose after he'd rubbished my cooking, when he'd only been teasing me and another time, squeezing his fingers that were sore from baseball, after he'd beaten me fairly and squarely at cards. He was always coming home with broken or sprained digits once he'd taken up baseball seriously and for a while, when I wasn't trying to injure him myself; I was bandaging him up.

Groves would simply give me one of his looks whenever the red mist descended and that was usually the signal for apologies and promises to control my wicked temper. And I honestly meant to, until the next time that is.

It was around this time that I started to notice changes in my body and as I had nobody to ask I just got on with things. By the time I was fourteen my period had started. I knew of such things from bits I'd picked up from older kids I knew, but the ever-faithful Mrs Maguire was my saviour. It didn't feel right asking Fanny, even though she was my flesh and blood, we were worlds apart in age and life styles and the last person I would have raised that most delicate of subjects with was old Groves.

In the end I took it in my stride and accepted the onset of womanhood the only way I could have done in the circumstances and got on with it as if nothing had altered.

But the winds of change were in the air and the events that took place on bonfire night of 1929, were to change my life forever.

5

It was the tradition in those days for every terraced street to have its own bonfire and as each street was a community in its own right, everyone who lived there attended, from the old to the very young, there were no exceptions. Neighbours roasted potatoes and chestnuts on the fire and passed around ale and homemade lemonade. They kept an eye on each other's children and if an adult from the street was to chastise a child for getting too near the fire, his Mother or Father wouldn't turn a hair.

I was fifteen and womanhood had begun to show on me already. My expanding chest pressed against my dresses and my body seemed to be changing every day. Groves spotted this too, but didn't say anything; he just left me money wrapped in a note one day that read;

Anne,
You're a woman now.
Use this money to buy yourself the things that a woman needs.

It was signed *Father,* but I knew old Groves couldn't read or write and therefore suspected this was in the hand of Mrs Maguire. I knew it wasn't Tommy's scrawl that's for sure and Groves would never have trusted such a personal matter with my giggling stepbrother.

Tommy often giggled like a girl when the mood took him and when he started, I swear it was so infectious that it would have made a Bishop smirk.

I had a good idea what I needed and did as the note suggested and it was at such times I was grateful for having old Groves. I was certain my natural Father would never have thought of doing the same in a month of Sundays.

My knowledge of things outside of my life in Liverpool was limited to say the least and whilst I could blame this partly on truancy, I did little to help myself, by reading nothing much more than the newspaper. That said, I'd always been mature in a lot of ways, but surprisingly innocent in others. People would call me streetwise today I suppose, yet I knew nothing of lovemaking and had no time for the dizzy day-dreamy love some of my friends confessed to experiencing. I was told by an older girl I only knew as Lilly who lived three streets away, that sex was what men wanted most of all in life. Another acquaintance, Marjorie Dunlop, told me that men wanted only three things from a woman; sex, children and food and according to her all involved hard work and very little pleasure for the woman. Another girl whose name I forget, told me that men's private parts expanded the more beer they drank and the only way they could return their organs to normality was to have sex for hours on end.

I found none of this helpful.

After all who could I ask about such matters, not Groves and certainly not Tommy? Fanny was always kind and attentive, but kept herself at something of a distance from me, therefore she was hardly somebody I could approach.

Contrary to most literature you might read, I knew I wasn't dying when the blood and cramps arrived. I just got on with it in private and found a way of dealing with the situation, with the minimum of fuss and disruption.

Yet all of the humiliation, the pain and confusion surrounding the advent of womanhood seemed worthwhile, when I first clapped eyes on the vision that was Angus Mackenzie Brown.

*

The fire was burning well and our neighbours from Harrogate Street were either huddled in their doorways, or stood in groups near the fire because it was such a cold night. The stars were all out and a magic quality seemed to fill the air, as I looked up to witness a slim uniformed figure, emerge from the entry connecting our street and Spurgeon Street. My eyes followed this stranger as he stopped to admire our fire. The flames danced in his dark eyes and as he drew close to the fire and removed his peaked cap, running the sleeve of his jacket across his brow, clearly feeling the heat. A broad smile seemed to light up his thin handsome face and I felt my knees weaken.

I couldn't take my eyes off him.

Then to my great surprise he noticed me too and still smiling he sidled up to me and just stood beside there, as if it was the most natural thing in the world to do. His close proximity seemed to turn my body against me, as my limbs grew heavy and my head felt as though it was made of cotton wool.

"The best one I've seen tonight," he said. His voice deep, carrying only the hint of an accent, indicating that somebody had taught this young man to speak properly.

Thankfully my voice didn't desert me when I needed it most and as I answered I prayed my reply would make sense, as my heart was hammering so hard against my ribcage that I was sure he'd be able to hear it over my voice.

"Y'should know by now that the best bommies are in 'arrogate Street," came my uncouth response, yet the nailed on smile still beamed back at me. Then from somewhere my voice spoke again, desperate to find a reason, any reason to make him stay a little longer.

"There's a spud or chestnuts going if you like, or if you're old enough there's beer."

I was intoxicated by his presence and would have jumped in the fire if he'd asked me to.

"Better not have any food my mam'll have my tea on and she'll play merry hell with me if I don't clear the lot, but I'll take a beer if you don't mind," he said.

Now it was my turn to smile. My smile was so big, I nearly tripped over it getting his bottle of beer from a communal crate, that was stowed in the shadows.

I handed it to him.

"Thank you."

"I'm Anne."

There was that smile again,

"thank you Anne."

We stood there as he sipped his beer and told me he was Angus and that he lived in Rishton Street which explained a lot. The houses were bigger there and the neighbours snootier. Mothers from Rishton didn't like their children to mix with kids from Harrogate Street in those days. He explained he was 19 and the reason he was wearing such funny clothes was because he was a chauffeur for the well heeled.

He could have been reciting his twelve times table for all I cared. I was captivated, enraptured and suddenly I knew what all the fuss had been about, when my friends talked about dreamy, mushy things like love. If this wasn't love I told myself, it must be the early symptoms.

Eventually he drained the bottle and my heart sank.

"Well goodnight and thanks for the beer Anne," he said and moved to leave, then stopped. "Oh I finish about four tomorrow and I always cut through Harrogate on my way home. I suppose I might bump into you if you're about."

"You just might." I replied, unable to stop the smile from filling my face.

Angus's Story - part 1

1

That bonfire night in 1929 was a pivotal moment in my life and little did I realise that the pretty brunette with fierce eyes would one day be my wife. She was much younger than me that was easy to see, but she already possessed a fine figure. As the flames danced in her eyes while we talked it, was impossible to determine that she had a blue and a brown eye. Many years later I read that Anne suffered from a harmless but extremely rare eye condition. But as I got to know her, I thought this typical of a young woman who demanded everything life could offer. One thing I did pick up on quickly was the strength of her character and even though it was very much a man's world back then, I doubted whether I, or any man for that matter, would ever tame her.

But I thought it might be fun trying.

We met the next afternoon and even though I was almost half an hour later than I'd indicated, she was waiting for me, although she was coy enough to wait for me tap her on the shoulder. She stood watching a group of children playing goose gogs, a game where they'd each take turns throwing a cherry stone up the drain pipe and once they'd rolled out, the furthest away cherry stone from the drain was the winner. She introduced me to her stepbrother Tommy who seemed an amiable enough lad and clearly thought the world of Anne. It was no surprise when I noted his fine physique, when she explained he played both the new sport of baseball and football, going on to tell me he harboured ambitions of turning professional at the latter. His grip was vice like when he shook my hand and he had the look of a thoroughbred, brimming with health and vitality, in a place that was less than healthy for the many of its inhabitants.

*

When I eventually made my way home, I remembered it was the night my my eldest brother James and his very pregnant wife Lilly had tea with us. I stepped through the door and noted everyone was present; Father, Mother, my brother Johnny, my brother Peter and my sister Marjorie, who we affectionately referred to as Margie. Silence greeted me as I crossed the threshold and the only other clue that I'd been the very recent subject of discussion, was a knowing wink and a grin from Peter, who was always full of fun.

I ran upstairs to wash my hands and face in a wash bowl of warm water Mother always had ready and as I ascended heard the hushed sound of conversation begin again.

I squeezed into my place and Mother and Margie served us. Once everyone was seated James cleared his throat and announced;

"Word has it that you were spotted in the company of a floozy from Harrogate Street last night Angus."

As he finished his sentence he glared at me, with a smirk on his face and although I told myself to stay calm, anger momentarily flashed across my face at his comment. James had this ability to get under my skin. Beneath my calm exterior, I was boiling with fury and hesitated, not able to trust myself by speaking, fortunately Mother interjected.

"Now James, you know quite well that Angus is an adult and who he chooses to spend his leisure time with is his own affair."

James coughed and tamely replied,

"Of course Mother."

Mother was an imposing figure, all 5 foot 12 inches of her. With never a jet-black hair out of place or a crease in her clothing, she had high standards and Victorian values, and James knew better than to tangle with her. Thankfully nothing more was mentioned about the subject, yet his derision of the residents from Harrogate Street troubled me. We were looked upon locally as better off than some. It was true our homes were slightly bigger than those in the likes of Harrogate Street and because of it our rents were higher, but ours were still only terraced dwellings when all was said and done. Perhaps it went deeper than that, it was only early days for Anne and I, but I detested the suggestion from my older brother, that she was somehow unworthy of our company.

Much later when James had long gone and the others were already in their beds Father and I were reading, he the *Liverpool Echo* and myself the *Evening Express*. I was still restless but I had to get up for work the next day and reluctantly stood and said goodnight to Father. Without averting his eyes from the printed words in front of him he said,

"Don't let them get to you *beurla* laddie.*"*

I smiled at his kind words and the use of his very own affectionate description for all of his sons. Its direct translation used the Gaelic word for English, coupled with the word laddie and as a Scotsman, it never ceased to tickle him that he had raised four English boys.

Father was born James Mackenzie Brown in Tillicoutry, a small village in Sterling, during November of 1878 and came to Liverpool to find work for the Mersey Docks and Harbour board, as an apprentice Cooper, eventually earning the hallowed title of Master Cooper, where he was known as Jock. He was a gentle soul, who was always pleased to hear a good joke and liked a drink when Mother allowed it. We often argued about football, as he followed Everton and I Liverpool, but that was how families were split in football terms and still are today on Merseyside.

Mother was born in Liverpool during September of 1892. Christened Emily Coffee, she came from a middle class background, hence her Victorian sensibilities. She was bombastic at times and believed in her own convictions and perhaps because of her strong personality, she was the undisputed head of the family. That said she had her gentle side and everything she did in her eyes was for the good of her family. She was also very creative, and made nearly all of her own clothes and always decorated our house, refusing all assistance and taking great pride in the results.

We lived at 84 Rishton Street when I was a child, but moved to number 87 when Margie arrived so she could have her own room. The result was, all of Emily Brown's precious sons roomed together. Fortunately once James moved out we were able to fit three single beds in the room at a pinch and as I tiptoed into our shared bedroom that night, I was relieved to learn Johnny and Peter were already both sound asleep.

2

James Mackenzie Brown Jr. was born in 1905 and was four years older than me. He was the spit from Father's mouth in every way, apart from colouring. Short in stature with jet black hair, contrasting Father's reddy brown. Both shared rounded shoulders and a knock-knee'd gait, but both were good looking specimens of the male race.

That's where their similarities ended.

Father was a gentle character, but my brother James was far from temperate. He was ambitious to the point of rudeness and enjoyed needling people. During my formative years, I was at the sharp end of many of his verbal wounds and learned very quickly to stay out of his way. It is safe to say James and I were never close, in fact we were worlds apart in our personal philosophies. He kept his own council and never shared his innermost thoughts with any of us. It was as though he had a chip on his shoulder, even though Peter once quipped it was more like a forest; I never for one moment understood why this should be. What on earth did my eldest brother have to be so angry about? He'd enjoyed a better upbringing than most in a working class Liverpool of the early 20th century and had done well at school. Good enough to secure a position at a snooty Gents outfitters known as Barnings. He eventually attained the position of Manager at another revered firm, Burmands Tailors; by the age of 21 years, earning very good money for a man of his age.

He was certainly an enigma.

By comparison Johnny, Peter and I were inseparable. John McIntosh Brown was born in 1907 and at two years my senior, was the tallest of the four of us. He also suffered at the hands of James, but being that little bit older, was better equipped to deal with it. I remember Johnny, known by some as Jack, was always well dressed and more often than not wore a pencil thin moustache, but removed it whenever the fancy took him. At the age of sixteen, Johnny found work at the Adelphi Hotel, which was a top-notch establishment in the second city of the realm in those days, frequented by many dignitaries and famous people of the day. I remember him telling me, he once waited on the famous Hollywood star Errol Flynn and a host of other stars of the silver screen, but it was not all a bed of roses for him. The year before I met Anne, Johnny suffered a nervous breakdown at the age of twenty, brought about by overwork they told us. Yet I suspected this was only partly true, as Johnny was a little too tightly bound at times and was prone to dramatic mood swings, even as a boy. The hotel accepted full responsibility and looked after him, sending him to a sanatorium in Grangemouth at their expense. It seemed to work as Johnny made a complete recovery and advanced to the position of headwaiter years later.

Peter who was also a McIntosh, was born in 1911. I was a Mackenzie like James and this was apparently to commemorate the two clans from where we hailed. English laddies indeed, who was Father kidding?

My abiding memory of Peter is of a lad full of mischief and fun. He also inherited Father's gentle nature and meant nobody harm in his constant pursuit of happiness. He'd torment poor Margie terribly, but she loved him dearly. She and I had always got on extremely well too and although she had some of Mother's ways, she had a much more tender side and I knew she had a soft spot for Peter and I. Peter was almost as tall as Johnny at around six foot and was dark like all of us, but he was painfully thin as a boy and Mother was always trying to fatten him up. God had also chosen to bless him with a prominent nose, yet it suited him and was a source of much of his comedy, by using his appearance as a prop. His occupation was less grand than the other two. He was a packer for a mail order clothing firm, but he also ran a credit drapery business, that started out as a very small concern, but eventually earned him more than all of us put together.

Margie christened Marjorie Emily Brown was not born until April of 1920 and in stature was a shorter version of Mother. Jack, Peter and I doted on our only sister. James was almost an adult when she arrived and had already married and left before she knew much about it.

Mother and Father never made a great fuss about it, it wasn't their way, but I knew they were truly content when Margie was born, they wanted a daughter and in the long run we all benefited from having Margie in our lives.

3

I was born on Christmas day, 1909.

Christmas of 1929 seemed to fly by and by spring of 1930 Anne and I were closer than ever. She'd recounted what she knew of her upbringing to me and I began to understand what had helped shape the young woman before me.

I was now twenty and Anne was not yet sixteen, but she grew more attractive to me as each day passed. We'd progressed to kissing and exploring each other's bodies, but we were able to restrain ourselves......just. My strict upbringing, combined with the idea that couples saved themselves for marriage in our day was a barrier to further exploration.

At the end of my shift each evening I'd park the Chrysler Sunbeam I drove for a living, then walk to Harrogate Street, where Anne would be waiting. I'd progressed to the inner sanctum by then, as Groves was not expected for at least an hour after me. If Tommy was not around we couldn't keep our hands off each other. Afterwards we'd tell each other the news from our day. Although the smell from the stove was inviting I was never tempted, as I knew I was expected to eat the meal Mother had cooked for me. Anne was still a secret from my family, and I was Anne's secret from Mr. Groves.

But that was all to end soon.

That evening we smooched for the regulation ten minutes. It was a full five minutes later as Anne was seeing to whatever was cooking and as I was leafing through Mr. Groves *Liverpool Echo,* the door suddenly burst open and in stepped a striking man, with a ruddy face, dressed in a jacket, scarf and heavy working boots. Although his bloodshot eyes were clearly startled by my presence, there was an intelligence behind his tired, illiterate stare and he'd quickly weighed up the situation and called to me,

"Evenin'."

I stood out of fright.

"Good evening Sir."

"Sit down lad," he told me, speaking down at the floor, as he struggled to take off his boots.

By this time Anne was standing red faced in the doorway, separating the kitchen from the front room.

"Ard day at work Father?" she asked. A lump the size of a dumpling in her throat.

"Not much different than usual lass."

"By the way," she went on, growing bolder and more like the Anne I was learning to love, "this is Angus. We've been friends for quite a few months."

His boots were off by now and he looked up and extended his right hand to me.

"Please t'meet ya lad. I'm William Groves, I expect she's told you what we are to each other. I can only say this though," he went on, taking an even firmer grip on my hand, "she may not be my flesh an' blood, but she means the world to me. I'd ask you to keep thar' in mind."

I remember standing awkwardly and saying something like,

"I feel the same way Mr. Groves. I'm extremely fond of your daughter."

"Don't' fuss lad," he told me. "Can you read that thing or are you just tryin' to impress me?" he went on, pointing to the newspaper I was still holding. "I never did learn to read. If you've any time to spare, I'd be grateful if you'd read a bir' of it for me."

"It'd be a pleasure Mr. Groves," I answered, starting to read the lead story with as much gusto as I could muster.

And that's how it began. From that day on if I was present when Mr. Groves came home from work, I'd read the *Echo* to him. Although Anne would sit on my shoulder as I did it, she was relieved that some nights I'd taken over a job she'd always found a chore. But I enjoyed reading to a man, I always found to be a real gentleman and if he ever had any reservations about me, he never showed them.

4

I suppose it was inevitable our relationship would reach my family.

Anne and I grew closer and more brazen in our relationship, until it reached the stage where we didn't care who saw us.

I still had not so much as mentioned Anne's name at home, but that was soon to change. It was a wet March evening of 1931 and our evening meal was served in what I can only describe as a subdued atmosphere.

Soon after the plates were cleared and the washing up done, everyone found their beds, which was highly unusual. Peter was the last to leave only Mother and I alone and his parting shot would have been funny in other circumstances, but his words made my heart sink.

"Who's been a naughty boy then?"

He winked and I must have looked back at him with a look of absolute horror. I made my way back to the sitting room, where I found my Mother knitting. She didn't look up as I sat in the chair opposite, to face the music.

"Mrs Lafferty is a good natured woman as you know," she began, "but she does have an uncanny ability of poking her nose into other peoples' business. I was disappointed to learn, she knew more about the goings on of one of my sons than I did."

I sat there in silence, my fingers digging into the arms of the old chair, waiting for her to get to the point.

"Low and behold if she doesn't tell me bold as brass, that my son Angus has been seen in the regular company of a young woman from Harrogate Street and then has the temerity to add, 'Mind you I wouldn't want my Tommy seen with anybody from that street.' Well I told her to politely mind her own business, but what I don't understand is why we're the last to know about this."

She locked her fierce, chocolate brown eyes onto mine and I felt like a small boy again, not a man of nearly 21 years. In truth though I did feel bad for deceiving my parents, but there was nothing for it now except honesty.

"Look I am sorry Mother. I meant to tell you, but I was worried you wouldn't approve and that's the only reason I've been putting off discussing it with you and Father."

"I do understand son, but now that it is all out in the open, I'd like to know more about your, erm friendship with this young lady."

I told her everything, how we met, how James had nearly given the game away and how I'd met Anne's stepFather quite by accident.

She considered what I'd told her, as I listened to the ticking of the mantle clock and the clicking of her ivory knitting needles.

"And what are your feelings for Anne?" she finally asked.

"I'm in love with her." I said looking down at the floor as though I should be ashamed of my feelings.

Her tone was softer now.

"Please believe me, I only want what's best for you when I say this, but I think you can do better than Harrogate Street. Goodnight now son."

She stood, put her knitting away, then kissed me lightly on the forehead and left me alone, with the impression she'd never accept Anne and the thought sickened me to my stomach.

5

The events of the previous evening were quickly forgotten, or so it seemed and Mother treated me just like the others at breakfast. Weeks passed and I began to wonder if it actually happened, but it quickly became clear how she'd decided to deal with it. Never once did she ask after Anne or her stepFather, it was as though she'd decided to ignore their existence, in the hope that they'd just vanish into thin air.

But the cat was out of the bag with the rest of the family. Johnny and Peter tried without success to embarrass me and find out as much as they could about Anne in the process, but I was tight lipped and unmoved by their attempts to wind me up. Only Margie showed me any empathy and she was just a month short of her eleventh birthday, when nobody else was around she'd always ask how Anne was and told me to ignore the others, assuring me Mother would come around in the end.

I only wished I could have been as certain.

Life returned to some normality. Summer came and went and it was soon bonfire night again, to signify two years since Anne and I first met. Anne was now seventeen and was slightly taller and leaner, but wider at the hips. Gone was any evidence of a child's body, every part of her was woman now and she marvelled when I looked at her with more than a glint in my eye. We were happy, happier than we'd ever been in our lives and that's how it should be when you're in love, but our happiness was to be tempered by the harsh reality and fragile nature of life. We looked to the New Year with hope and love in our hearts, little did we realise that 1932 was to be one of the blackest my family would ever face.

*

Christmas and New Year went by without so much as a word to me about Anne and another savage winter gave way to a spring, a season that was almost wasted on the inhabitants of inner city Liverpool in the thirties. Unless we ventured into the park, there were no daffodils growing nearby, no blossom trees for us to marvel at, no lambs bleating in any nearby fields, the milder weather was our only gauge to work with. In fact thinking back, spring and autumn were often the best months living the way we did. We often struggled to warm our houses in the winter, but found them unbearably warm at times during the summer.

Summer of 1932 was soon upon us and it brought the usual warm weather, but the worst of news. Lilly, my eldest brother James's wife turned up on our doorstep around teatime, Sunday 10th July, with her daughter Jean tucked up inside her pram asleep. Lilly was in tears and it took Mother and Father over half an hour to get any sense out of her, she was so shaken up. Father plied her with a large measure of his Johnny Walker whisky, as Margie watched over little Jean, who slept through it all. Lilly was eventually able to tell us all that James had been complaining of a pain in his right hand side for over a week, but refused to see the Doctor.

"He's headstrong Emily, you know that."

"He's my son alright," Mother agreed, outwardly in control of her emotions at least.

"Well, he went off to work today as usual, but he looked pasty faced and moved slowly, like he was in a lot of pain. I begged him to go to the Doctor again, but he said whatever ailed him would pass. But he was wrong. I received a message from the shop boy only an hour ago, telling me that he'd collapsed at the store and they called an ambulance and had him rushed to the *Royal Infirmary*."

"And what do they say is wrong with him?"

"I don't know, but I've got a bad feeling about this Emily, very bad."

"Look now, you've got to be strong for Jean. James and I will accompany you to the hospital right away and we'll get to the bottom of this. Angus go to the top of the road and hail us a taxi."

"I'll do better than that, I'll go and bring the Sunbeam around."

"Now Angus you can't risk losing your job we'll manage."

"No this is different Mother, they'll understand. Now get yourselves ready and I'll run and fetch it."

6

I waited with the car and my parents led Lilly through the doors of the infirmary, their faces taut with nerves.

When they emerged over one hour later I knew it was bad news, I put the paper down and looked across at the three figures in the still bright June night. My Father, whose shoulders were already rounded, walked out with a positive slump in his posture and looked as though he now carried the weight of Liverpool on his shoulders. Mother's pale mask gave little away, but I knew she was working hard to keep her emotions in check. Her arm was around the diminutive Lilly, whose face was buried in her handkerchief.

They climbed into the car without so much as a word. I started the engine instinctively and looked across at my Father who'd climbed in beside me. His face had a crumpled and defeated look.

"It's bad son, very bad," he almost whispered, as a single tear burst from his right eye and he put his hand to my knee as if to comfort me. My body was in a lather of sweat as I headed the car back to Harrogate Street. I took the occasional glance at my Mother, although her expression was impossible to read.

A Victorian to the end.

I climbed out of the car in a daze and after letting my passengers out, I followed them inside totally numb from head to toe.

Mother assembled the family together in the sitting room and as they took their seats, I stood in the doorway and listened to the words my Mother calmly trotted out, as though she were reading a knitting pattern aloud.

"I'm sorry to report that James is gravely ill. The Doctor tells us because James was untreated for appendicitis, his condition worsened and his bowel has perforated. I believe the medical term is peritonitis." She paused to exhale deeply and then took a deep breath before continuing. As she did both Lilly and my Father could be heard sobbing in the kitchen. "The Doctor has been very open with us and I'm grateful for it. But he has told us he will be amazed if James lasts the night. I am very sorry to be the bearer of such bad news children."

Margie ran to Mother and they embraced. Peter looked down at the floor and Johnny looked across at me, his eyes brimming with tears, but then he'd always shown his emotions just like Father.

I was dumbstruck and sick to my stomach.

Still holding our sister to her bosom Mother spoke again.

"Father and I will accompany Lilly back to the hospital to wait at his bedside and to pray for a miracle. Try and get some sleep if you can and we'll get word to you as soon as there is any news."

We trouped out again and it was now getting dark.

We made our way to the hospital in silence; each of us wrapped up in our own thoughts. I parked in the exact same spot as before, hardly anybody drove in those days.

I accompanied them inside this time and the sterile smell of the place filled my nostrils. My parents knew the way and I followed a few paces behind. A nurse spotted my Mother and hurried to her side and I stood at my Father's side as the nurse spoke to her in a hushed voice. The nurse left and Mother turned to us, her appearance now grave.

"He needs blood. They want to test us to see if any of us are a match. If the three of us don't match up perhaps you could bring the others here Angus?" she said, then stopped as though confused. "It's just that a transfusion is his only hope you see."

In that moment my Mother let her mask slip and I saw a woman terrified out of her wits. Father saw this too and placed his arm around her waist and led her forward.

"Come on then Emily, we'll do what they ask."

We were each tested and I was found to be a match.

They led me to my brother's side. He lay on his back, clearly sedated, his skin looked to have the texture of marble and I couldn't take my eyes from him as they arranged everything.

In those days they transferred the blood directly from the donor to the patient and the process was painstakingly slow.

*

When it was over they gave me a cup of sweet tea and a biscuit and insisted I drank and ate before I was allowed to leave.

My parents met me in the waiting room and after giving them details of what had taken place, at his suggestion my Father and I walked outside to take in some fresh air.

After meaningless some small talk, he took he took my hand in his and said,

"You go on home and get to your bed. We'll find our own way back son. Besides you've done more than enough."

I nodded in agreement, but as soon as he was out of sight I climbed into the back of the Sunbeam and stretched out on the rear seat, but every time I closed my eyes the face of my brother James and his daughter Jean stared back at me. I don't know how long I lay there, but I suppose I must have eventually fallen into a light and fitful sleep.

*

A light tapping on the car window woke me and I opened my eyes to a bright morning, my eyes quickly focusing on a dishevelled shape standing hopeless and tear stained in the morning light. I staggered out of the car and took hold of my Father.

"He's gone lad. Gone from us. Why him lad? God almighty, he was only twenty bloody six years old."

I held my Father close and a feeling of guilt coursed through my very being. My eldest brother was lying dead in some nondescript hospital room and I was still breathing. I'd never even liked him, nor understood him for one instant, but blood is thicker than water and my mind could not absorb the fact that I'd never lay eyes on James Mackenzie Brown again.

7

The funeral was difficult on all of us and this will come as no great surprise, given the premature nature of my brother's death. Perhaps because of this, plus his young age, our plight touched the local community and his name was on everybody's lips for weeks.

I fancy he might have liked that.

Mother cried all day. No matter how strong she undoubtedly was, no Mother expects to outlive any of her offspring. It was the blackest of days and I was in no hurry to repeat the experience. After the funeral, Mother laid on some food on and we ate, but she quickly found her bed, unable to face a moment more of it. Margie kept an eye on her, as we took hold of Father and shunted him outside.

We had other plans for him.

Only men frequented pubs in those days and Johnny, Peter and I whisked Father off to the *Richmond* in the hope of drinking him and each other into oblivion. I discovered both of my remaining brothers were suffering similar feelings of guilt to my own, because of their own poor relationships with James. None of us could admit to liking him, but love is a different matter and as the beer flowed and our tongues started to loosen, we recalled tales from our childhood, things we'd almost forgotten.

In the *Richmond* word quickly spread we were intent on drowning our sorrows and before long we were unable to put our hands in our pockets to buy a drink. The generosity of our friends and neighbours was astounding. For all the hardships people suffered, working class communities pulled together at times like this and it seemed that every man who lived locally attempted to buy a round of drinks for the Browns in their hour of need.

We staggered home more than the worse for wear and though not a man or Jack of us was physically sick, we'd supped some ale between us.

It was just enough to numb the pain and although Johnny and I were steaming drunk, we were able to help Father out of most of his clothing and settled him in the lounge, before noisily tiptoeing to our own beds.

I went to see Anne the next day.

8

Anne had suffered loss and disappointment in her own life and knew words wouldn't help me feel any better. Drawing on her experiences I knew she needed time to recover from the shock of my brother's sudden death.

But her solution was to fuss over me. She must have taken me in her arms over a hundred times that next day, but I didn't complain about it once. I was suffering true enough, but partly due to imbibing enough mild beer, guaranteed to bring many a strong man to his knees.

Mr. Groves was appropriately sombre and offered his condolences. Tommy shyly did the same, but in truth it was the most they could do, it was impossible for them to understand my emotional state. In a way I was experiencing feelings of guilt for not making more of an effort to get closer to James and troubled by the fact that no matter how hard I tried, I couldn't think of one kind or thoughtful thing we'd ever done for each other. We were like two ends of the same ship, never able to meet.

It was soon Sunday and Mother had insisted we all attend nearby St Benedict's church as a family and pay our mutual respects to a God, who had for some reason found it necessary to take her first born. Now some might think the decision I made took advantage of my Mother's delicate state and perhaps in a small way that was true - but there was another reason. James's death had a profound effect on all of us, yet it forced me to consider the fragility of life and to focus on my own mortality. For me there was no question of hiding Anne away in the next street anymore. She was the woman I loved and my Mother could like it or lump it. I didn't know how long my life would be, but I was sure of one thing, I was going to live it and enjoy what I could of it with Anne at my side.

My Father seemed more inclined to join me and my brothers at the pub after James had passed on, no longer caring whether Mother approved or not and Johnny who had always been a little uptight seemed to relax more in the months that followed. Peter remained his usual amiable self, as did Margie, but once or twice I happened upon each of them deep in thought.

Mother was deeply troubled by the whole experience and gained the least from it.

She came around in the weeks that progressed and was once more the stoical head of the family and although she and I had always enjoyed a close and affectionate relationship, in the coming years our feelings for each other would stand the sternest of tests.

When I asked Anne to join me that evening at church, her face went as white as a sheet and she began to flap like a bird, whirling around the terraced house in Harrogate Street, wringing her hands.

"How can I Angus? What will I wear? An' your Mother she'll 'ate me."

"She won't hate you," I assured her, secretly hoping I was right. "And just wear whatever you…erm….usually wear to Church. Besides it's about time they get to know you."

That stopped her in her tracks and she smiled warmly at me.

"Is this becomin' serious?"

As if she didn't know.

"Will you tell your daughter that it's been serious since the day we met William."

Mr. Groves laughed at that.

"I reckon she already knows that lad."

*

She looked stunning in a dress I later learnt was a hand me down from her older sister Fanny. It was ivory in colour and fit her lovely figure as well as the pretty lace gloves on her hands; the outer layer a mass of brocade. She'd tied her long brown her into a bun and pinned a hat to the right side of her head at a slight angle.

I was so proud of her for fighting off her obvious nerves. I'd crowed often enough about my Mother's implacable strength and Victorian values and this must surely have played on Anne's mind, although she didn't say so. When she took my arm, she trembled ever so slightly, but taking a deep breath she found strength from the reservoir of resolve she possessed. Off we went, proud to be in each others' company, making our way through to Rishton Street, the ringing endorsement from Groves helping us make the final few steps together.

"My goodness Anne you look a proper picture, if only I had one of those photographic contraptions I could mark it for posterity."

But I didn't need photography; her sparkling eyes, her full mouth and her tiny hand upon my arm were indelibly fixed in my mind.

I'm not sure whether my Mother was fully aware of Anne's presence that night. She was pale and distant, yet we'd broken the ice. The others made up for her reserve, by making Anne feel as welcome as possible. My brothers nudged me from time to time, winking and giving me the thumbs up. Margie had a knack of sensing what a person needed and she was on hand to help Anne when we returned home for sandwiches and Dundee cake. She was never far from Anne's side, not crowding her mind you, but doing just enough with an encouraging word here and there.

Father pulled me to one side and I could smell the malt whiskey on his breath.

"She's a real looker son and although she hasn't said much, I can tell she has a real spirit. You've done all right for yourself with this one Angus. Just don't let her get away."

I said very little and remember grinning inanely, but it was a cause of great relief for both Anne and myself. We'd climbed a mighty hurdle that day and although we weren't quite on the home straight, the going at least for now looked good to firm.

9

Time moved on and another birthday I shared with the King of the Jews arrived. Before I knew it I was 23 years of age and it was 1933.

By January 30th of that year a little known individual had become Chancellor of Germany and although it was hardly commented upon at the time, by the end of March of that year he'd set up the first concentration camp at Nuremburg, just outside Berlin. The little known Adolf Hitler had also passed an act giving him dictatorial power by March 23rd. Yet, none of this was reported upon in any detail and subsequently it was given hardly a passing glance by men and women reading their daily newspaper.

Anne and I gradually became comfortable in the company of my family and she was a fixture at our gatherings for Sunday lunch, along with Lilly and baby Jean, who Mother doted on. Yet I sensed Anne was wary of my imposing Mother and I'd noticed they'd never in fact spoken directly to one another. My Mother either didn't want to get to know the real Anne, or was playing a patient game of sizing her up. Either way I didn't like it and the longer it went on I secretly grew more anxious.

Soon it was spring and Anne and I accompanied Johnny and his girlfriend Ethel to New Brighton on one of his rare weekends off. Peter and a girl he was fond of, Elsie Flowers, invited themselves and we caught the tram to the Pier Head and boarded a ferry to take us across the grey waters of the Mersey. The girls all wore headscarves in an effort to stop their hair blowing everywhere in the breeze that blew across the open river. They wore their best summer dresses and the chaps wore jackets and ties. Johnny was his usual dapper self and outshone Peter and I. I remember how on the journey across the Mersey, we all stood and watched the long white Pier at New Brighton come into view, excited by the prospect of our day out.

New Brighton was a typical seaside resort in the thirties with a promenade, a regular Punch and Judy stall, candy floss, indoor bingo and row upon row of drinking establishments. We did all the usual things, then put a penny in one of the telescopes on the prom and looked across at the Liver birds perched above Pier Head and further along to Albert and Kings Dock. We soon got hungry from walking and a thirst for something stronger than lemonade on sale along the way. Johnny knew the owner of the

Grand Hotel, who was happy to be our host and at his suggestion, we made our way there with our girls on our arms. It was one of the few places where a respectable lady could enjoy a beverage with her beau in those days, as long as she avoided inebriation.

Johnny's friend was the Headwaiter and took us through to a private bar reserved for residents and special guests. Johnny arranged for sandwiches and our first round of drinks arrived on the house. Anne had never before tasted alcohol and at my suggestion tried a gin and tonic, but didn't care for it much and nursed it for most of the time we were there. Peter and I joked and teased the girls, but his joking went a little too far with Anne and perhaps he hadn't realised at the time how short her fuse was, or how explosive her temper could be. He took a plate of sandwiches bit into all of them and switched them with Anne's when she visited the ladies' and asked in a rather loud voice why she'd want to take a bite out of each and replace them on her plate.

She exploded.

The fire in her eyes was a sight to behold and at one point she seemed ready to physically assault him, standing and lurching toward him, until I grabbed her hand and pulled her down beside me.

"He's teasing you Anne. Don't let Peter's clowning get to you that way."

I was smiling to mask my acute embarrassment, but Peter and the others seemed unmoved and laughed it off.

"It woulda served you right if she'd walloped you one," Elsie told him.

And it was then that Peter gave Anne a name he would always use and it stuck.

"That's some temper you've got their Dagger."

"Dagger, who's Dagger?" Anne asked.

"Why with a temper like yours Anne, that's the only name I can think of calling you."

"Oh take no notice of him Anne," Johnny called out, "he's always been a bit soft in the head, I think Mother dropped him once or twice."

We all laughed and then laughed some more as Peter pulled one of his faces in answer to Johnny's remarks.

It had been one of those perfect days and by the time we stumbled out into the fresh air, a cool wind had whipped up. We gallantly offered our jackets to the girls and made our way to the ferry terminal.

As we waited, Johnny put his arm around Ethel and announced that they were to be engaged and told us Ethel had agreed to marry him the following year. We passed on our congratulations as the ferry came into view, but before we boarded, Johnny turned and added,

"We haven't told Mother or Father yet, so please don't mention it."

Of course, Johnny - who doted on Mother - had realised in a lucid moment, if she'd learned we'd been told before her, it just might have an adverse affect on their strong relationship.

10

Mother gave Johnny's marriage to Ethel her blessing and they were married in November of 1934.

By this time, Hitler had opened Dachau concentration camp and had passed a law decreeing that the Nazis were declared the only party in Germany. And, seemingly unnoticed by the rest of the working class population of Europe, the Germans withdrew from the League of Nations. If that wasn't bad enough the Nazis were responsible for the murder of Austrian Chancellor Dolfus in the early part of 1934, although no blame was attributed to them right away. Then, shortly after the death of German President Hindenburg on August the 2nd, Hitler declared himself the Fuhrer of Germany.

It was around this time that Anne and I talked about getting married and having a whole football team of kids. It was foolish talk, the talk of two people hopelessly in love, yet it was proof we both felt our engagement and eventual marriage was inevitable.

Johnny and Ethel's wedding was at - where else but - the Adelphi Hotel, where he'd decently acquired the exalted position of Headwaiter. It was there under a great glittering chandelier with the taste of real champagne still on my lips for the very first time, I proposed to Anne. She accepted with a deep exhalation, so strong that it was as if she'd been holding her breath for months waiting for me to pop the question. She smiled at me through moist eyes, taking my face in her hands and kissing me full on the lips and it was the sweetest kiss I'd ever experienced.

"Yes Angus. I'd be 'appy to be your wife," she told me.

We held each other and nothing else seemed to matter, the world was she and I and not even the recent death of my brother could spoil it.

*

Our happiness was dented somewhat when weeks later we announced our engagement to Mother and Father. Mother's face was set like stone as she replied,

"And you've thought this through Angus? You're certain Anne is the girl you want to marry?"

My Father looked across at her, his mouth half-open.

I was slow to catch on, too wrapped up in my high emotional state and I answered smiling.

"Of course she's the one for me."

"Very well then," was her less than overwhelming acceptance of our union.

Looking back Anne's weak smile spoke volumes, but I didn't see any of it, I was blinded by my own happiness.

*

We set our wedding day for Boxing Day of 1935, a day after my 26th birthday and I thought this was just about the perfect birthday present. We were to move in with Groves until we could find our own place. Tommy had recently married Lilly, somebody we hadn't known much about until his marriage was announced, Tommy certainly was a dark horse. He and Lilly now had their own place a few streets away.

Christmas came and went again and I welcomed the New Year by looking for a better paying job and found one at Taylor's bakery as a delivery driver.

Mother seemed critical of my every move during that period and she was most unhappy that I'd given up my poorly paid chauffeur's job, for what she considered to be a poor alternative at Taylor's. This surprised me as my new job paid considerably more and for me driving was not real work. I loved to be behind the wheel of any kind of motorised vehicle and it was something I knew I was good at. I'd been blessed with excellent co-ordination and just like my future brother in law, who was a natural athlete, I believed I was a born driver.

The new job suited me down to the ground. I was driving and meeting a variety of people throughout my working day and as somebody who loved to socialise I quickly made lots of new friends. I was also able to bring home sweets and bread that hadn't sold. The bread went to Anne, along with half of the sweets to satisfy her sweet tooth, the other half went to Margie who was growing into quite a young woman. She was blessed with Mother's strength and yet she'd somehow gained Father's tact and humility.

She may only have been 14 going on 15 in 1935, but she could see what Mother was up to and she was our strongest ally in the dark days that followed.

11

It was around the time Mother announced our cousin Elsie Lewis was getting married, things started to go wrong. Elsie, it seemed wanted Margie to be her bridesmaid, and realising the pair had never got on, I glanced across at my sisters's reddening face, expecting her to object. But she held her tongue. She knew better than to tangle with Mother across the dinner table and in the presence of her finest crockery and silver serving implements.

Mother went on and on about Elsie's wedding and how wonderful it would be, why it was likely to be the event of the year in our family.

I narrowed my eyes and looked across at Anne who was now fidgeting with her food. Her first-rate appetite seemed to have deserted her and in her eyes there was a fiery look as she threw her fork down onto her plate. The conversation died and everyone turned in her direction. She glared at Mother. Johnny and Ethel looked horrified, even Peter who'd invited Elsie Flowers for the first time looked concerned. James's wife Lilly looked down at the tablecloth seemingly unable to cope with what was unfolding.

"Excuse me Emily," Anne said at first, a slight tremor in her voice. "Bur' 'ow can the weddin' of your niece be the event of the year when your own son is gettin' wed in the same year?"

Mother paused, wiped her mouth with her napkin and fixed her eyes on Anne. Her expression impossible to read.

"Now you know very well Anne that what I said was a figure of speech." She came back meekly and it seemed for a moment that she wanted to undo any damage. A collective feeling of relief quickly passed around the table and Anne seemed to breathe for the first time.

But then the bombshell came. She clearly couldn't let it go at that.

"That doesn't mean of course that I'm thrilled by your pending union with my son."

It was the spark to light the blue touch paper. Anne's combustible temper detonated. She stood up sharply, upsetting the crockery by banging her leg on the table.

"I knew it!" she roared, as the red mist fell all about her, "you've never liked me from the very first day I set foot in your precious 'ouse, you with your 'oity, toity ways. To you I'm no better that the dirt on your shoe."

"Come on Anne, nobody's saying that….." I broke in, but my efforts were useless.

"You never gave me a chance, not one."

It was my Mother's turn to stand now and her imposing figure cast a shadow across the table.

"And you wonder why when you behave like this, after you've been invited under my roof. This is how you repay a kindness is it Anne?"

I was concerned by what might follow, but it seemed the flames had been doused by my Mother's last comments.

Instead Anne looked across at my red face.

"Angus will you walk me 'ome please?" she asked, but this was no question I could say no to. I grabbed our coats and in a moment we were out in the cool night. I put my arm around Anne as she began to cry and told her it would be alright, but then I knew the stubborn streak that ran through my Mother.

"I don't care what she says about me…..but she…..she shouldn't talk about your weddin' day….like that……it's not right Angus."

I had no answer and one thing was for sure there would be no quick fix.

12

It was 26th December 1935, the day of our wedding day and most of my family were absent. Mother had not forgiven Anne and had decreed there would be a family get together as usual on Boxing Day and everyone was expected to attend. Quite what she thought when Margie got herself ready and made her way to St Benedict's church I'll never know. Cut from the same impenetrable cloth as Mother, my baby sister possessed genuine metal.

Peter would have been my choice as best man, but Tommy Davies was an able and willing stand in and I said little about my family's no show to Anne. It was a slap in the face to her, what with only John and Fanny representing her blood relatives. The way I looked at it though, this was Anne's big day and nothing; not even the childish behaviour of my parent's could change that. I was determined they weren't going to ruin it for her.

I was thinking that very thought when I turned to look up the aisle and feasted my eyes on the beauty walking towards me, on the arm of William Groves. The thin sinewy strength of the blacksmith was never more evident, as he walked with Anne, he was light on his feet and seemed to move with the grace of a dancer; enjoying every moment of what was surely the proudest moment of his life.

There was a fabulous spread laid on at Groves's home, with contributions from the entire street. There was dripping sandwiches, cooked hams and blocks of cheese, plus homemade apple and rhubarb pies. There were also jars of pickled walnuts and gerkins. On top of which was a healthy supply of booze, from whisky and gin, to crates of brown ale and Stout. I carried Anne over the threshold to what was also to be our home for the next couple of years, as we waited for a suitable place of our own to become available, and the waiting neighbours clapped and cheered us.

Inside we were surprised to find a rather sheepish looking Johnny and Peter, standing stiffly beside their respective partners, Elsie and Ethel.

It seems they were expecting some verbal tirade from me, but I was never happier to see them both and held my arms out and the three of us hugged briefly. Johnny was smiling widely, but for Peter it wasn't enough, he felt as if he needed to say something.

"Angus we wanted so much to be there, but we......"

"Look I understand. You're here now and that's all that matters. Anyway, when are you going to congratulate the new Mrs Brown," I said, smiling in the direction of an equally pleased looking Anne. They hurried to her side as Margie came in behind them. She came to me quietly and threw an arm around my waist and stood on tiptoe to kiss my cheek.

"Well done."

She looked close to tears.

"No, thank you. I'll never forget what you did for me today," I said and meant it.

Without warning Johnny barged his way in between us, having regained his composure. Margie stepped away from him and went to find a home for her hat and coat, never a great advocate of Johnny's in those days, finding him a little too full of his own self-importance at times.

"Before I forget," he said rummaging in his inside pocket and extracting a bulky brown envelope, "I need to give you this, from all of us," he went on, pressing the gift into my hand. My mouth dropped open when I peeked inside to reveal the princely sum of fifty pounds and instantly realised what the phrase 'all' of us meant.

"I'm very grateful for this Johnny and please don't doubt my sincerity, when I say I'd give all of this up to make it right between Mother and Anne."

"Oh Angus," it was Peter the optimist talking now, "Mother'll come 'round and you know it."

I said nothing, but nodded as I tried to imagine how the two most stubborn women in Lancashire would give ground. I found the prospect unlikely, but that was for another day.

"Have you told him about the other thing?" Peter asked Johnny, quickly changing the subject.

"Not yet, I was saving the best 'til last," Johnny answered. "There'll be a car arriving for you and Anne," he said, stopping only to look at his watch. "Let me see, in about two hours. I've pulled a favour at work and got you a room at the Adelphi for the night, but don't thank me, it was Peter who put me up to it."

I smiled at my brothers and said,

"Well I'll drink to that," reaching for the brown ale.

*

It was a bittersweet night of emotion I would never forget. And as Anne and I lay in our matrimonial bed and held each other, little did we know that other troubles threatened to destroy the life we so gleefully mapped out together in whispers, as we lay entwined. Hitler had not only violated the treaty of Versailles by introducing military conscription during 1935, but he'd also stripped Jews of their human rights by invoking the Nuremberg Race Laws.

Still the Europeans and our press gave him very little space on their broad-sheets, even as whispers of the persecution of the Jews gathered pace, the news agencies, together with world leaders, refused to believe the claims. How could one human treat another so disgracefully they all asked? How indeed.

13

Mother continued to keep Anne and I at arm's length as the New Year progressed.

I used to meet Peter at the pub every Thursday evening to catch up on the family news and sometimes Johnny if his shift permitted. We'd meet up at either the *Richmond House* or *Cabbage Hall* usually, both close to *Anfield* stadium, where once *Everton* played, but was by then the home of *Liverpool*. Often our discussions would turn to the troubles in Europe, but we weren't the only ones. The male population of Britain was growing uneasy as more and more stories appeared in the papers referring to the escalating troubles in Europe, but nobody dared speak the word that was on everyone's lips.

That dirty word was War and I suspect the reason for this was that memories were short. Almost every family from that era lost at least one male relative in the Great War and it was never supposed to happen again, but it seemed that a day didn't pass when there wasn't something new happening in Hitler's Germany.

In February of 1936 the Gestapo were placed above German law and in March, Hitler's troops marched into the Rhineland. Mussolini's Italian forces took a leaf out of Hitler's book by marching into Ethiopia, as the ugly face of Fascism began to spread its terrible cancer across the world and as always happens, the working man was set to pay the price. A man who toiled to put food on the table with little time for any strong political or ideological views, but the same man who is always the pawn of the worlds' powerbrokers.

Like most working men I tried to put any thought of war out of my mind and mostly succeeded. I was a newlywed and liked to rush home to my bride after work and tell her about my day. We'd usually wait for Mr. Groves and all eat together, but one night in February Anne served me one of my favourite meals of white fish and boiled potatoes, before William arrived home. I knew from Anne's face that there was something on her mind and then as she told me my heart lifted,

"I'm pregnant Angus."

It was what we both wanted and I pushed my plate aside and took her in my arms.

"Oh Anne its wonderful news. I love you so much," then cupping her stomach in my hand I said, "both of you."

*

Our elation was quickly dashed when Anne miscarried. There was nothing I could do to console her for weeks, but eventually she accepted my theory that it was nature's way of telling us there was a problem. It didn't deter us, or stop Anne from dreaming of Motherhood and creating a dynasty of her own and something tangible for her to hold onto.

But as the year moved on, we returned to the rhythm of existing from day to day and little did we know that there was worse to come than the loss of our unborn child.

By July of 1936 Anne was pregnant again and our thoughts were once more focused on the future. This time Anne was healthy and as she grew larger, remained rosy cheeked and energetic, cooking and keeping house just as she did before. 1937 couldn't come quick enough as far as we were concerned, but how wrong could we be?

14

Civil war had erupted in Spain during July of 1936 and by October Franco was declared head of State. Hitler had done nothing more than host the Olympic Games in August of that year, but all of it passed us by. We were in a world of our own. Even the ongoing impasse with my parents couldn't spoil our happiness, but an incident in February of 1937 did and would leave an indelible mark on me for the rest of my natural life.

As I've mentioned previously, it was a pleasure to drive in those days, with hardly any other vehicles on the road and I couldn't think of a more enjoyable way of making a living.

I remember it was a cold February day and I was making my usual deliveries on Sleepers Hill, a route I knew like the back of my hand, when without looking a female child standing at the roadside, suddenly lurched out into the road directly in front of me.

She'd either been oblivious to me or had something else on her mind.

I knew the instant she moved into my path I'd never stop in time, yet I pushed the brake down with every ounce of strength I could muster. It wasn't enough and if I'd tried to a thousand times I would never have been quick enough.

The sound of her fragile body colliding with the bread van made a sickening sound and chilled me to the bone.

It was a split second I would never forget my whole life.

I climbed out of the van in a dreamlike state and a woman wearing a winter coat and a headscarf was screaming. I ignored her at first and forced myself to look.

Her tiny body was off to one side. She looked like a rag doll, her form in an unlikely pose for a living creature, but of course she was no longer living.

The child was dead and I'd killed her.

*

The Police arrived quickly followed by an ambulance, although I never learned who summoned them and all the time I sat at the curb side staring at the lifeless form, until she was carried away and into the ambulance.

The screaming woman had not been her Mother, but instead a neighbour of the child's family. She told the Police I was completely blameless, explaining how the child had bolted out in front of the van, leaving the driver no hope of stopping.

But it was cold comfort to me.

The Police Officer was a big strapping Irish sergeant, who sat down beside me at the roadside and spoke to me softly, aware of my distress.

"Angus none a dis was your fault lad, I'm absolutely clear in me mind. But a want you to come wid me t' the station and make a statement. The sooner you get dis lot out a your head and down on paper, the quicker d'healin' process can start."

"Right Sergeant," I answered, rising to follow him to his car.

He stopped and turned to me, his grey eyes fixed on mine.

"No Angus, I want you to follow me in the van."

This woke me up.

"Are you mad? Look at me," I held my shaking hands out in front of him. "I can't drive with these things."

He took a step toward me, his expression flat. Placing his meaty hands onto my shoulders he spoke to me slow and deliberate.

"If you don't get back into dat van and follow me, you'll never drive again. Now do as I say."

He turned abruptly on his heel and found his way into his car and started the engine up, never once looking back at my frozen frame.

I remember standing there confused and stunned by the recent turn of events, but eventually I fumbled at the van keys in my pocket and gingerly climbed back into the cab. I'd never been so terrified of anything in my whole life. He waited a couple of minutes then started the Police car up and moved off. I reluctantly started the van with trembling limbs and followed at a more than safe distance.

I now know the officer did me a great favour that day, had I not done as he had insisted, I doubt whether I would ever have driven again.

*

Mother somehow got word of what had occurred and she and Father appeared on Groves doorstep that same evening and as he let them in, hot tears streamed down my cheeks for the first time that terrible day.

Mother approached me and took me in her arms.

"She was so tiny, so tiny and her little face. Oh Mother if I live to be a hundred I'll never forget it."

Much later William Groves, myself and Anne sat with Mother and Father and talked together, as if the two previous Christmases had not passed without so much as a word between us. Then as they stood to leave, Anne walked forward and embraced my Mother, thanking her for calling. Mother's face softened for the first time I could recall in Anne's presence.

"When is my grandchild to be born?" she asked.

"Sometime in April."

"Then I expect to see a lot of you both between now and then."

"You will."

Whether Anne's well meant comments were for my benefit I'll never know, but it was finally over. On the worst day of my life, Anne and I were finally welcome amongst my family again.

15

Our son was born on 10th April of 1937. We called him James after my Father and eldest brother and like all newborns he had bright blue eyes that would ultimately turn brown. He was a lusty, healthy boy child and we doted on him. And it always amazed us how as our first born grew, he came to resemble his genetic namesakes, something that constantly left me in awe of nature's way. Facially he was so like my brother and physically the same build as Father. In fact his coming helped ease some of the pain I still suffered in silence, when I thought of my eldest brother's short life and that poor child who'd died under the wheels of my van.

I'd smoked my way through double the number of cigarettes between February and April, in addition to my consumption of alcohol that also increased. But when James arrived all of that changed. I drank less and even started to smoke a pipe in an effort to reduce my tobacco intake.

The troubles in Europe seemed to escalate through 1937 and on into 1938. In November of 1937, Hitler revealed his war plans during the Hossbach Conference. Then in March of 1938, a union with Austria was agreed, just prior to the mobilisation of the German military machine. If newspaper reports were true, the combined military strength of a Britain and her European allies was no match for the Germans. It worried me that if our press were right, then surely Hitler's advisors knew it too.

The entire Country held its collective breath when Neville Chamberlain met with Hitler in Munich during September and returned waving that now infamous slip of paper, claiming to have appeased the madman. My brothers and I were still concerned as reports reached us that the Germans were planning to march into Czechoslovakia. We were not made to feel any better by the news that the Czech government had resigned in October of that year.

*

I met with Peter, Johnny and my Father at the *Richmond* for our usual Thursday night drink in October of 1938 and the atmosphere was sombre. A feeling of resignation seemed to have enveloped the male population and I believed I was in the grip of an incredible force I had no control over and a war in Europe seemed unavoidable.

Johnny was adamant he'd join up the moment war was declared.

"Hitler's a monster and a tyrant and needs to be taught a bloody lesson," he said, slurring his words.

"We'll see about that if the time comes," Peter said.

"When the time comes?"

I looked across at Father, who hadn't spoken for some time. His eyes were moist. He caught my gaze and wiped them with his sleeve.

"Come on Father, don't take any notice of those two. They won't let it happen again."

"I wish you were right *beurla-laddie*, but I fear that your brother's correct. This madman has to be stopped and I see nobody but us standing up to him."

We managed to pour more whiskey down Father's gullet than ever before that night and the three of us carried him home as he was no longer able to stand, much to Mother's disapproval.

On my way home I tried my best, but could not shake the heavy burden of impending doom and felt stone cold sober by the time I climbed into bed.

James Brown (Angus's eldest brother)

James and Emily Brown (Angus's parents)

Anne's Story - part 2

1

The war was all some people talked about and I was no worse, badgering Angus at every turn.

"Will there really be a war?"

I don't know why I pressed him so often because he'd always become agitated and pull his nose out of *the weekly news* or *the Evening Express* and look up to me shaking his head.

"I just don't know love," he'd say, wringing his hands and usually reaching for his pipe. I was always sorry I'd driven him to it, but I couldn't help myself. I had to admire his stamina for reading about it for hour upon end though. He'd read every reference to war in every paper he could lay his hands on and although he didn't share everything with me, he'd often put the paper down and stare off into space, pale faced. I never knew whether this was with anger or fear, but I suspected a bit of both. With all that he read I often thought he must be the most well informed man around and I don't think I was far off, as a good deal of the men folk living about us were no great scholars, a bit like me I suppose.

At meal times while little James was napping, we'd share any news and inevitably Angus would pass on little titbits about the problems in Europe. He was enraged in January of 1939 when Hitler was reported to have threatened the Jews in a now infamous speech and he was no better when in March, the Nazis marched into Czechoslovakia.

Deep down he didn't want to tell me any of it, but I think it was troubling him so much that he just had to get some of it off his chest. Towards the end of March news reached us that the Spanish civil war had ended and although none us hardly dared take a breath things seem to calm down a bit. Although I bet the people of Czechoslovakia wouldn't agree with that.

*

We'd quickly slipped back into the routine of visiting Angus's family and our long disagreement was never mentioned. I found that odd, as this way of brushing things under the carpet was alien to me and would never be my way of handling painful or unpleasant things, I'd rather have one final slanging match and get everything out in the open, but I was forced to accept it was the way the Browns dealt with such things.

To be more precise it was Emily's way.

Initially I approached the imposing head of the Brown clan warily and I can't speak for her, but I'd say we tip toed around each other in those days leading up to the war. I never shared any of this with Angus though. He was so pleased to be back in the bosom of his family and I couldn't spoil that. I took the view that as long as she was civil with me I would hold my tongue. She wasn't somebody who'd show strong emotions, but her face would light up whenever she caught sight of our son.

Angus and I had never made any secret of our wish to start a family right away and in early 1939 we announced I was pregnant again, during one of Emily's dinners. Everyone assembled was suitably overjoyed. This pregnancy felt different and as I grew bigger the bump seemed smaller, or maybe it was just my imagination? Mrs Maguire who was one for superstition and other mumbo jumbo, assured me I was carrying a girl, boys were big out front was her view.

"It's a girl Anne, I guarantee it," she'd say, whenever we passed in the street.

I remember lying in bed around early spring, over two thirds of the way through my pregnancy. James was sleeping peacefully in his crib and I could hear Angus breathing deeply, soundly asleep. I smiled to myself, daring to dream that I might have my own little girl soon, a child who unlike myself would always know her Mother.

I intended to make sure of that.

2

Apart from something Angus referred to as the pact of steel, the Nazis had signed with Italy sometime in May of '39, news from Europe was scarce and as I reached the final weeks of my pregnancy I was filled with optimism for the future. Surely sanity would prevail. Hitler would come to his senses and remember the horrors of the Great War he'd been part of.

Our daughter Emily was born on a sunny Saturday on 29TH July of that year. The weather was glorious and the birth was a good deal easier than it had been with James. Mrs Maguire insisted I stay in bed for a week as I'd done the first time and everyone fussed about me. Angus's Mother fed us all that week and Groves joked that her cooking was certainly an improvement. I'd never liked sarcasm and as the red mist descended, I just missed him with my hair-brush as he ducked out of the room, a mischievous grin on his face.

Once I was up and about I was proud to parade my son and daughter around and about. Often at the weekend we took the tram to Newsham Park and if we were feeling adventurous we'd venture further afield to Sefton Park. It was closer to the City Centre and a short walk from Otterspool promenade, on the banks of the Mersey and handy if we fancied a walk along, to cool down on warm Sundays. There we'd linger after our picnic and watch the local toffs stroll out of their mansion houses that looked out over the park and prance about in their fancy clothes, never daring to cast a glance over at us ordinary folk sitting on the grass in our Sunday best. Little did they know that the class system they belonged to was about to die a quick and painless death. Yet as I sat with my man and our two babes, never happier in my entire life, I dared not consider that the walls of my own private bliss were about to come tumbling down.

*

During August of that year the pressure valve burst and matters spun out of control. Like most of the citizens of this small island, I felt very much like a helpless bystander, watching and waiting on the sidelines, as matters beyond my understanding or control unfolded.

On August 23rd Angus explained to me that the Russians had signed a pact with Hitler. Nice of them I thought, failing to really grasp the significance. This was followed swiftly by a treaty of mutual assistance signed between the British and the Polish Governments and Angus explained what that meant. He told me if Germany invaded Poland, things would start to happen fast and in my stupidity, I didn't quite realise at the time, that this single act was the catalyst for what was to follow.

By the end of August the British military fleet was mobilised and civilians were evacuated from London, yet I still didn't really get it, but he did. His Thursday night forays with his brothers and more often than not his Father, were less like a quiet drink and more like a series of drunken binges and I still didn't really know why.

The point was Angus knew what was coming. But he also realised it was coming like a high speed train, none of us could stop or derail.

On the 1ST of September 1939 Germany invaded Poland and by the 3rd of that month we were at war. We, France, Australia and New Zealand declared war on Hitler's Germany.

3

I tried to convince myself they wouldn't want Angus because of his age. He'd be 29 by December. They'd want the young men first and by then it would be all over, but of course in my private fantasy I didn't count on scores of men volunteering for the forces the moment war was announced. Johnny was one of them and I feared my man would follow suit.

Soon after signing up Johnny called 'round with Peter and his Father to announce his decision and although it was a Tuesday evening the men went off to the pub, even Groves and our Tommy joined them. I couldn't rest for a moment when they were out and busied myself with housework that didn't really need doing, imagining the lot of them marching through my front door and proclaiming they were all joining up, even Groves and Angus's Father.

I was worrying myself into the ground when Angus found his way inside, quickly followed by Groves, who saw my face and quickly announced he was off to bed. Angus sat beside me in front of the fire and even though I could smell the drink on his breath he looked sober and serious.

"How are the children Anne?" he asked, staring into the fire.

"They're both asleep, although Emily'll probably wake for another feed in a few hours I expect," I answered, as we both skirted around the issue.

"Was ar' Tommy okay with the drink and everythin'?" I went on, remembering my stepbrother drank very little compared to Angus and his brothers.

"He was merry that's all. He doesn't try to keep up with us. He's a good strong lad and smart too, he doesn't say much but he's a good listener. I expect he's just the sort the enlistment Officers will look out for. Our boys are dispensable despite what they say and I tell you Anne, they won't be satisfied until all of our brothers and sons are out there risking their lives for King and country."

It was then that I noticed there were tears rolling down his cheeks.

"Does that mean you won't be followin' Johnny's lead?"

He turned to me; his eyes rimmed red with tears, reaching out to cover my hands with his.

"I want to. I feel as though I'm obliged to, but then I look at our children and I can't. They need me here."

I moved closer and took him in my arms. It was what I wanted to hear. I kissed him passionately and took his face in my hands.

"I need you," I told him, moving onto his knee and allowing my dress to ride up to the thigh. He dropped his hand onto the bare flesh of my leg and my skin tingled and as we kissed again and I knew that need didn't even come near to the love I felt for him.

*

As early as the 4th of September there were reports the Royal Air Force had attacked the German navy in the Atlantic, to begin what was a six-year war of the waves. It was no surprise to anyone that Churchill who had just been made Lord of the Admiralty, following the swift formation of Chamberlain's war cabinet was behind it. It was his style to strike the first blow and even then it was clear that if anyone ever had a purpose in life, Winston Churchill had found his vocation. To have him in our corner at a time of crisis was something to cling to. Angus had told me often he'd been a singular voice against the Fascists in Germany and had campaigned in Parliament, urging MPs to prepare for war.

The word locally was that Britain and her allies at that point were ill equipped to stand up to Hitler and it was widely anticipated the Americans would join us, but our hopes were dashed when they proclaimed their neutrality on September 5th. Canada however joined the allies on September 10th, but seven days later there was more bad news when the Soviets marched into Poland.

Angus continued to scour every newspaper report he could lay his hands on and began to smoke and drink much more, as the strain began to take a toll. I did my best keeping a good house, looking after the children almost single handedly, and cooking his favourite meals of fish and scouse, but he was preoccupied totally by the thoughts of war.

Each night as I put the children to bed I looked at their innocent faces and braced myself for what was to come.

4

1939 ended with a series of events that drove Angus to distraction. It began on the 27th September when Poland surrendered to the Nazis and by the 29th the Soviets and the Nazis were dividing the Country up like it was a cake, each nation hoping to gobble up the biggest piece. In October, news filtered through that Hitler was planning to kill sick or infirm children under the age of three and what was labelled the Nazi euthanasia program by the British press, was soon expanded to include older children if reports were true. We were unsure whether this was merely part of the propaganda war when further reports told of human experimentation on the children.

On 8th November of 1939 a Swiss clock maker who had worked in Germany for several years and bitterly resented the Nazi stranglehold on labour unions, decided to kill Hitler. He went by the name of George Elser and had he been successful, millions who would perish might have lived on. Unfortunately Hitler's spy network caught wind of the plot and the Fuhrer suddenly ended a speech he was giving in the Burgerbrau Beer Cellar and George Elser was arrested much to the free world's regret.

As if that wasn't bad enough, the Soviets then marched on Finland during 30th of November and by December 14th they were expelled from the League of Nations. This prompted Angus to announce the world had gone mad and I could do no more than shake my head and agree with him.

*

Our first Christmas at war was drawing near and peace on earth and good will to all men was something that seemed to have been forgotten. It should have been a time of great delight for Angus and I. We had our little boy and our little girl and were about to move into our own home in 17 Harrogate Street that had recently become vacant, but a giant shadow hung over us all.

That said, we did our best to forget the war, but it was difficult. Angus with the help of Peter, occasionally his Father and even old Groves, decorated every room in the house. It was no more than a lick of paint, but it brightened the terraced house up no end. Our family and neighbours, to add to our meagre possessions donated various bits of furniture.

It seemed every Harrogate Street resident was determined to play some part in our move. If they weren't helping us lift something inside, they were passing food or drink across, or a bucket of coal. People were different then, salt of the earth and as I've said before the street was a proper community. Even though the likes of Rishton street still looked down on us, from their slightly larger houses, their neighbours were just the same as ours.

We spent Christmas day morning at home, opening gifts and playing with the children. Before lunch we collected Groves and went on to Angus's parents' for Christmas dinner. This was to be Johnny's last Christmas before starting his basic training in the New Year. For that reason alone the day was tinged with sadness and when Angus would normally have been the centre of attention because it was also his birthday, that honour quite rightly passed to Johnny. I remember Emily making a particular fuss of him that day, and to be fair to her she had never ever shown any favouritism toward any of her offspring. But Johnny welcomed her special attention, as he totally doted on his Mother. She could do no wrong in his eyes.

That was to be one of the last occasions we'd all spend together for a very long time and as I looked back on the laughter and the gaiety that ensued, it was a million miles from the trauma to follow.

Rationing began in early January of 1940. Up to that point it was a daily visit to the corner shop, some things simply didn't keep in the larder. Mr Grant our local shopkeeper knew it was coming and complained in the months leading up to rationing that he just didn't have enough goods to sell. The rules were that we had to register with a butcher and a grocer and hand over our Ministry of Food ration books to each shopkeeper, who would remove the necessary coupons. I remember that I didn't think we'd ever survive on the meagre weekly ration we were allowed. For each adult it was something like;

> 3 pints of milk
> Margarine or butter - 4 oz.
> Sugar - 8 oz.
> Tea - 2 oz.
> Cheese - 4 oz.
> Cooking fat - 2 oz.
> Bacon - 4 oz.
> 1 egg.
> Meat to the value of 1 shilling and two pence.
> Sweets 3 oz.

Allowances altered as the war rolled on and some foods become impossible to get hold of. People were encouraged to grow their own vegetables and posters were plastered everywhere starring Potato Pete and Doctor Carrot. I seethed whenever I saw them because it was impossible for us to grow anything. We only had yards, although some of Angus's customers with gardens started to grow their own produce and on the odd occasion, a generous soul would hand him a bag of fresh veg. I don't remember what the allocation for potatoes were, but thanks to my husband's contacts they were something we could almost always get hold of. I could therefore still make scouse and when meat was scarce, I often made blind scouse as it was called. This was a stew without meat. Angus as I've indicated also loved fish, but that was one foodstuff that virtually disappeared during wartime, at least in Liverpool. Even though we were a port, the black market was soon the only place to get your hands on decent portions of fish and you needed a letter from the Pope to get anything at a decent price.

We were forced to find new recipes with the ingredients at our disposal and I remember making potato pancakes from a little milk, carrots if I could get any and some salt and pepper, although I occasionally threw in some cheese. It was impossible to buy a large quantity of meat, unless you had a contact on the black market and bucket loads of money. We had neither, therefore I made things like cheese soup or cheese and onion that was baked in oven a bit like a flan. As you can tell we had plenty of cheese and as a result it went into almost every meal.

Another thing we quickly got used to was carrying our gas masks everywhere. Even James and Emily were issued with a mask that was a bit like a bag, with big round eyes and a nose piece and it was thought the kids looked a little like Mickey Mouse when they wore them. Adult masks were somewhat bulkier and cumbersome, but thankfully there was never any call for us to wear them. It seems that Mr. Hitler missed a trick when he forgot to try and gas us.

In every street, bomb shelters were put up and the plan was that the ordinary people from every street would travel to the dingy foul smelling shelter, whenever the air raid signal sounded. In the days and months that followed, some would refuse to leave their homes and escape without a scratch, others would not be so lucky. In Rishton Street where earnings were greater, some families invested in Morrison shelters when they were available from 1941. They were basically a stout table with a large metal block fixed on top. The idea was that the family huddled beneath it during an air raid. They were said to have saved families whose homes collapsed around them. Those with gardens had Anderson shelters put in, although I wasn't to have the pleasure of using one personally until much later in the war.

Blackout was another imposition. During the hours of darkness no light was allowed to escape, to prevent the Jerries from seeing their targets, after all we didn't want to make it easy for them. All street lamps were extinguished during darkness, making the outside world a treacherous place to navigate on a cloudy or moonless night. To help, lampposts were painted white and large white lines were painted to separate the kerb from the road, but despite this people were injured or even killed. Some were struck by vehicles with special shields over their lights designed to release only a limited amount of light, making it impossible for unsuspecting pedestrians who might have wandered into the road, unable to see an oncoming vehicle.

Let us not forget the blackout warden, who could fine you if your home was not properly blacked out.

In the early days of the war there were many changes for us to come to terms with, but at least I had Angus by my side.

What I didn't know was for how long.

6

By March of 1940 Finland had successfully repelled the Soviets and a peace treaty was signed between the two Countries, yet as any good news came our way it was followed by the inevitable bad news, as the Nazis bombed Scapa Flow naval base near Scotland. The bombing of Britain had not quite arrived as it had been expected and we were thankful for it, but it seems that Hitler was occupied invading Denmark and Norway during April. Following this up with the invasion of France, Belgium, Luxemburg and the Netherlands in May.

It was 10th May when Angus jumped for joy in the lounge and I almost dropped Emily from the shock, as he was never so animated. I thought for one fleeting moment the war had ended, quickly realising how impossible that was at the time. Germany had Europe in a virtual stranglehold and they were clearly winning the war. But my husband's joy related to the war in a way. It had been announced on the wireless, that Winston Churchill was to be made Prime Minister and it was exactly what we needed according to Angus.

Holland surrendered on 15th of May 1940, resulting in the evacuation of allied troops from Dunkirk and quickly following on the heels of the Dutch surrender was the submission of Belgium. Angus like most men of his generation watched on helplessly as Hitler brushed aside our European allies with what seemed to him, consummate ease. Next Hitler was bombing Paris in what was a relentless drive to expand the German Empire and as Norway surrendered and Italy declared war on Britain and France, it looked increasingly like we were isolated. Marshal Petain became the French Prime Minister, but Angus wasn't fooled by this and sure enough France signed an armistice with Germany four days after Hitler and Mussolini met in Munich, on 18th June 1940.

The Soviets were still busy while all of this was going on, beginning their occupation of the Baltic States.

Angus smirked when Churchill announced that Britain recognised General Charles De Gaulle as the true leader of free France, stating that nobody was fooled by Hitler's occupation of our European neighbours. He also sighed and looked into the dead fireplace, due to the warm summer air and said,

"We're on our own Anne. Only we can stop him now. Thank goodness for the English Channel."

On July 10th, the battle of Britain began and Hitler was to suffer his first bloody nose in his relentless march on Europe. He was unexpectedly stopped in his tracks, but a lot was to happen in between.

The children had been fed and changed and Angus and I settled down to listen to *Band Waggon*, featuring *Arthur Askey,* on the wireless. Before it started he took my hand and turned across to me.

"There's talk at work all able bodied men under 40 will be called up. I think we should prepare ourselves."

I tried to be strong, but tears filled my eyes, as almost a year of hoping against hope disintegrated, making me a hopeless blubbering mess.

"It'll be alright Anne. Come on now. Those lads at work are probably only pulling my leg," he said, trying to comfort me, when it would be him putting his life on the line.

He was wrong of course. Within a few weeks he'd received his call up papers and if he passed his medical he'd be taken from me on the 12th of September 1940.

7

The months leading up to September seemed to fly by.

It seemed somebody knew of his skill behind the wheel of anything mechanical, as he was posted to join the Royal Artillary as a driver. Before that though he was obliged to take a medical and I won't deny I hoped he'd fail it. I didn't think he had flat feet and I knew he didn't suffer from asthma, but I hoped they'd find something like a tiny heart murmur, anything that meant he'd stay with me and out of harm's way.

He passed with flying colours of course. I remember him coming home that afternoon after spending most of the day waiting his turn and true to form he'd already started making friends. He regaled me with tales about the boys he'd encountered and this was no loose language. In his opinion the so called men who were soon to be his comrades at arms, were nothing but children.

"Most of them have known nothing of life at all Anne. One chap was so scared he wet himself. Another lad so impoverished he didn't have any under garments. I only hope Mr. Hitler has no inkling of what we're massing to face him. An army of old men and children," he said, shaking his head and walking from the narrow kitchen to where James played with some wooden blocks in front of the fire. Our son turned to look up at his Father and instantly a smile of recognition flashed across his three-year old face. He stood and ran to Angus and flung his pudgy arms around his legs. Angus plucked him up from the ground and into his arms.

"Hello son, have you been a good boy for your Mother?"

"Yes daddy," he answered, but his attention quickly skipped and focused on the block he was holding. On it was a faded letter S and on the opposing side a Crimean soldier, with rifle and bayonet at the ready.

"Let me see son," Angus said, taking the block from him and turning his head to me, "no wonder there's war when we give our kids things like this to play with. Let's hope my fellow soldiers realise quickly this is for real and that they'll need to do more than play at being bloody soldiers."

With that he dropped the block to the floor and James looked down at it forlornly as Angus hugged him tight to his breast. Emily suddenly gurgled in her pram as if she realised her sibling was receiving all of her Father's affection.

*

There were many things to think about before September came around. One was to decide what would happen to us in a worstf case scenario, but each time Angus raised the subject I'd either burst into tears or engineer an argument. I couldn't and wouldn't dare think about his death. As has been well documented already, I have a terrible temper, but I was also a stubborn bitch when the mood took me and in the end I think I wore my poor husband down, so much so that one Monday evening he took old Groves to *Cabbage Hall* for a drink. When both presented themselves at my door some three hours later, merrily swaying before my eyes, they pushed passed me arm in arm and stood before the fire, still holding onto each other for dear life.

"It's been discussed Anne," Angus announced.

"Yes it's been agreed," Groves seconded him.

"Whar' 'as?" I asked, growing perplexed.

"The subject, the one you won't even hear talk of."

"Now look 'ere," I said, feeling my dander rising.

"Stop that young lady," Groves sternly cut in and I must say it was the one and only time he'd ever raised his voice to me. I was stunned into silence. "No daughter of mine will speak in that tone to her 'usband. As Angus 'as stated, the matter has been discussed, duly agreed upon and is now closed. Now your inebriated 'usband and I will retire for the evening. After you Angus."

"Thank you William," he replied and smiled his gorgeous smile at me as he made his way to the foot of the stairs. Groves letting himself out and off the short distance to his own home. I watched them both in stunned silence.

I never did find out what they'd agreed.

8

A number of people conspired to make our last night together a special one.

Angus said his goodbyes to his work mates and by all accounts there wasn't a dry eye at *Taylor's* on his last day. My husband loved the company of others and had clearly worked his magic at his new place of work, just by being himself. That said, there was perhaps more of an edge to it when somebody was called up. It was human nature after all to wonder if you'd ever see a friend or work colleague again.

I cried enough tears to fill a dozen tin baths, but none of it altered the fact that my man, the love of my life, was soon to wrenched away from me. He'd soon learn how to kill people, but more importantly to avoid being killed.

I was a wreck and might not have retained my sanity without the kids to care for.

Emily insisted that she'd take both her miniature namesake and her older brother off our hands on the Sunday before he was due to report for enlistment at Kinmel Park in North Wales. Angus and I discussed it and agreed that the children would stay with us for the day, but we'd let them sleep over at his Mother's.

The weather had been turning cooler of late, but the anticipated Autumn weather suddenly turned and something of an Indian summer took hold that weekend. We decided to take our chances and headed for Sheil Park on foot. Angus carried James on his shoulders and I pushed Emily in the glorious sunshine. This type of outing was frowned upon because of potential air raids. But we didn't care, we were enjoying our last day together the way we wanted to. To any unsuspecting passer by I'm certain we'd have looked like a typical family on a Sunday outing, they couldn't know that the smile they saw on my face was nothing more than a mask. My insides were churning away like a rusty old mangle, but I wanted Angus to have his last day as a happy memory. I had no idea what he'd face in the months ahead, but I was shrewd enough to know he was likely to come across some unpleasant situations, to say the least and when he was feeling low, I wanted him to know what was waiting for him at home.

Thankfully there were no air raids to trouble our thoughts and although Sheil wasn't our favourite local park, it was close and we found a nice spot for Emily and I to sit on a blanket and watch

James and his Father play football. At one point my eyes filled up as I watched my little boy playing happily with his Father and felt Emily pushing herself upright and yelp with joy as the boys played right in front of her. She so much wanted to join in and it would come as no surprise that she'd be the street tomboy as an older child, never happier then when she was playing cricket or rounders with the boys. Both she and James were oblivious to the fate awaiting their Father, or the absence from him we all would be forced to endure.

Try as I did, I just couldn't slow the clock down and time elapsed much quicker than I wanted it to. When Angus needed to catch his breath we all sat and shared a Dundee cake Groves had been hoarding, washing it down with no more than a bottle of tap water.

"Come on Anne, let's get the children home, I can feel the temperature dropping," he told me, smiling his delicious smile again and I asked myself, how he could he be so brave?

He took his jacket off and draped it over my shoulders, confusing the goose bumps on my arms with a subtle change in the weather, not realising it was my high emotional state. Yet the jacket enveloped my body with the smell of him and my senses were immediately calmed by the sensation. James and Emily were in the pram together at this point and despite Emily rubbing her eyes before we left, she was now wide awake at the prospect of being close enough to touch her older brother, who was gentle with her, despite her rather heavy handed prodding of him.

Angus slipped his arm about my waist and we both pushed our siblings' home, my head occasionally falling onto his shoulder.

What was I going to do without him?

*

His Mother was waiting as we reached Rishton Street and scolded us for keeping the children out in the cold, quickly ushering them both inside. As she did, his Father pressed an object into Angus's hand.

"What's this?"

"It's a little something I've been saving *beurla-laddie*."

Angus unwrapped it and announced,

"This is fifteen year old whisky Father? Are you sure about this?"

"As sure as I am that you'll make us all proud son."

I watched on as the diminutive figure took hold of his son, his eyes brimming with tears as he kissed Angus on the lips. Then he turned on his heel and said,

"I'll see you both in the morning."

The door closed on us and I looked across at my husband whose bravery was now being tested to the limit.

We walked hand in hand down the familiar path to our home and as we reached the door, he lifted me into his arms.

"It's about time I carried you over the threshold Anne. I did it at old Groves place, but not here, why didn't you remind me?"

We made our way inside and as he made up a fire, I quickly stepped out of my clothes and opened my arms to him

*

The whisky was two thirds empty and as we lay entwined in front of the dying embers of the fire, a plate of cheese crumbs beside the whisky bottle, I looked into his stunning brown eyes and run my fingers through his hair and spoke,

"D'you think there are men all over the country saying goodbye to their sweethearts and wives right now?"

"Most of the men in my regiment, if they can be referred to as men, will have been tucked up by their Mothers hours ago. But I suppose there will be those whose girls will be making sure they have something to remember them by."

I pulled him close to me.

"Will they make sure three times?"

"Three, but......"

I pushed him onto his back and moved on top of him and kissed him, wanting it to last forever. Wanting a memory of my own if truth be known and as our passion grew, a small part of me cried out in vain, protesting against the madness and futility of war.

'Why are you leaving me, it said, why now when I need you the most?'

Angus in uniform

Johnny (Jack) Brown in uniform

Peter (to the right) in uniform

Tommy Davies in uniform

Angus's Story - part 2

1

Hundreds of men and women came together on the draughty platforms of Lime Street station. Even though it was Monday, little James and Emily were all done up in their Sunday best and looked bemused, although I think my three year old son had an inkling of my going away. When I knelt down to kiss him, he looked into my eyes and held them for a moment,

"We'll be okay Daddy, but in case you're bored I want you to take this," he said handing me a beaten and scratched die cast toy tram William Groves had given to him and it was all the more poignant because this was his favourite thing in all the world.

"I'll only take this if you're sure. After all, I I know how much you love it. Look why don't you keep it safe for me until I come home?"

But my boy was stubborn like his Mother and even at a young age he rarely changed his mind once made up, even if the decision saw him suffer personally.

My sweet little Emily was totally oblivious and as I took her in my arms and felt her tiny hands on my face, the touch and feel of my darling baby girl almost brought me to my knees. Yet Fathers all over this island were leaving the ones they loved so that we might all be free and although I knew I was doing the right thing, knowing it didn't make going through with it any easier. I kissed my daughter for the last time and reluctantly passed her back to her Grandmother, who true to form was an absolute rock. I kissed the white makeup that always covered her face and knocked her knitted hat slightly askew and unlike her, she kissed me back vigorously and whispered,

"Don't you be worrying about Anne or the children. With William's help, your Father and I will keep them safe. You just come back to us in one piece."

I turned to Father who was crying again and we held each other in a great bear hug for a few minutes, but he said nothing. What would you say to your son in such a situation? I couldn't possibly contemplate what it might be like sending my own son off to fight. William Groves shook my hand and his blacksmith's vice like grip nearly crushed my bones.

"We'll all be fine son, you just come back to us."

"I'll do my best William."

I turned to Anne, who'd never looked more beautiful to me, even though she'd had no more than a couple of hours sleep. She looked calm and radiant and almost pleased to be seeing me off, but her act didn't fool me. She was holding herself together for my sake and as I took her in my arms, I was almost lost for the second time in a matter of minutes. I expected floods of tears from her, but they didn't come, at least not in my presence.

I held onto her until the last possible call, then grabbing my case I took flight on feet made of lead and jumped aboard, turning to watch their faces as the train moved off. There were smiles and frantic waves and as the train turned sharply and they were lost to me, I was suddenly deflated, forlorn. It was as though the umbilical cord to the life I knew and cherished had been cut and nothing but the great unknown awaited me.

The journey was uncomfortable and even with all of the windows open the smell of sweat and cigarette smoke hung in the air and filled my lungs. I reached for my fags and decided that if I couldn't beat them, I'd join them. I was lucky I found a seat in a cramped carriage, as the central passageway was crammed with testosterone in all shapes and sizes. Some were fortunate enough to have made friends or were travelling with people they already knew. There were quiet chaps too, who clearly didn't want company, but more than a sprinkling of gregarious types, happy to share a joke or an experience with their fellow conscripts.

I would usually have fallen into the latter category, but I was happy at first to watch the nameless railway stations fly by, having got myself a window seat. The odd thing was that the MOD's decision to remove signage from all railway stations to make life difficult for the enemy in the event of a land invasion, meant that we had no idea how much further our journey would last. Although I understood the reason for the decision, to me the stations now seemed lonely and isolated places stripped of their identities.

About an hour into the journey the silent passenger immediately to my left stood up and vanished without a word and I never saw him again. In his place an enormous man who was easily six foot six inches in height, squeezed his frame between myself and another chap.

"Sorry," he said, as he struggled not to crush us with his gigantic thighs. I turned back to my tattered copy of *Titbits* and tried to ignore him, still in no mood to talk, but it was difficult as his massive chest wheezed like an old stove.

2

The landscape started to change before my eyes and despite my age I'd never been much of a traveller and had never journeyed much further than the end of my nose. That might seem strange, but in those days people didn't generally move about much. I'd been told how fabulous Welsh scenery was and I put my magazine down for a moment and marvelled at the beauty of the greenery and wide-open spaces before my eyes.

"Good read?" the giant asked me.

I was still a little stunned by the view and it took me a moment to realise somebody had spoken.

"Bits of fluff and nonsense really," I said, "but it helps to pass the time. Would you like to borrow it? I'm almost done."

"No thanks. My eyes are a bit tired, maybe later. I'm Ted Willis by the way," he went on, extending his big hand in my direction. I didn't have the wit at the time to realise the man's eyes were not the problem. The answer was staring me in the face. Like many adults from that period, big Ted Willis was illiterate and could not read.

"Gus Brown," I said, shaking his big hand briefly, "I take it you're on your way to Kinmel Park too?"

"Fraid so. Royal Artillery Light anti aircraft."

"Me too."

"I just 'ope there's plenty a grub. I'm starvin' already."

Looking at him I suspected he'd eat enough for four men and that was without a day's regular exercise, how hungry was he going to be once he was shedding pounds?

*

We disembarked at another unmarked railway station around lunchtime and waited around for about one hour, before we were herded aboard a fleet of trucks. We arrived at Kinmel Hall late Afternoon. The hall and grounds were impressive. The house was built from sandstone and was more than twice the length of Harrogate Street in width. Built in 1870, to replace an earlier mansion destroyed by fire in 1848, Kinmel Hall and nearby Gwrych Castle had been the principle employers in the area for many years. In fact the owners bought land from each other to prevent development of the area. As a result nearby Abergele lagged behind Colwyn Bay and other seaside resorts of the day.

Although the place was certainly eye catching, as a City boy I found the quiet unnerving. I did eventually grow used to my rural surroundings, particularly in the evening when the constant grind from the city seemed a million miles away and a man could settle on his own thoughts in relative peace and quiet.

We were told the place had been used by the army during the Great War to train raw recruits and had housed the military on its grounds since 1930.

We were quickly organised into our regiments and billeted in small huts. It was eight men to a hut and I was pleasantly surprised to discover that Ted Willis was not only in my regiment, but was to share the next bed. To his great relief they fed us next and the food wasn't half bad. It was a stew that had plenty of meat, potato and vegetables and this was perhaps not surprising given the rural setting we found ourselves in. The army had clearly struck up some sort of a deal with the local farming community who were still able to produce the same quantity of foodstuffs, but could no longer trade on the open market.

Not a great deal happened for about ten days until we were kitted out with battle-dress, a large back pack and another smaller pack, webbing, a respirator, a heavy overcoat, a standard issue steel helmet that weighed a ton and assorted field-dressing. We were also issued with identity tags, kit bags and boots although mine were two sizes too big and had to be returned. Poor old Ted had a bigger problem though. Nothing he was issued with would fit and almost all of his kit was re-ordered. Some weeks later we were all issued with our own .303 Lee-Enfield rifles and their arrival had a strange affect on some men. Some saw them as a new toy and greeted them with delight, others like myself were a little less enthusiastic. I knew my new rifle had been engineered to kill people and the thought of it did little to foster any warm feelings from me toward the thing.

Our training began in earnest once we were dressed like soldiers and we were expected to wake at six, shave, wash and dress ourselves and make our own beds. This was proceeded by thirty minutes of quite vigorous exercise before breakfast and when you consider the majority of the men were young and reasonably active for most it wasn't a problem. I on the other hand was approaching my 29th birthday and although I'd always been slim and reasonably active, I drove for a living, plus I smoked and drank too much. I told myself that this was going to be hard and I wasn't wrong.

3

A chap billeted with us who went by the name of Hobbs, liked to tell stories and I got the impression he embellished them quite a bit. He claimed there were riots at Kinmel Hall during the Great War and the place was smashed up. He went on to claim he had it on good authority hundreds perished and as a result, over fifty men were fcourt marshalled and subsequently killed by firing squad. He used this tale to claim the top brass were nervous about lightning striking twice and we should use this to our advantage to try and improve our conditions.

"Well you seem to have it all figured out," I told him, winking at Ted, "we'll leave it to you to do our negotiating with the brass then shall we?"

Strangely he didn't raise the subject again.

I was to learn much later there had indeed been a riot in 1919 to be precise. It happened when the place was inhabited by over 19,000 battle weary troops, most of them Canadians. The conditions were thought to have been atrocious, with little food and not enough facilities. The riot claimed the lives of five men and injured others and there was a court martial, but no record of mass firing squads.

Once we'd reached a minimum standard of fitness brought about by long cross country runs, our entire regiment moved to nearby Sennybridge, a Royal Artillery training camp. We were shown how to put up regulation tents and to arrange and camouflage them in such a way that afforded us protection from possible airborne attack. This was how we lived for six weeks despite the cooling October temperatures, but we realised we needed to prepare to live this way in preparation for the looming theatre of war that awaited us.

The place was vast and consisted of bog like land when flat, with pretty streams and wooded areas dotted about, all in the shadows and silence of the hills all around us.

I could put up with most exercise but detested the assault course, mainly because of the uniforms we wore. The deliberately boggy ground under netting where we were expected to crawl on our stomachs soaked our kit and the material just sucked the moisture up like a sponge. If it was raining, a man could expect to carry double the weight of his pack, trying to complete the course. It was around this time that we learned how to shoot our Enfield rifles and I was surprised to find I was a reasonable shot, considering I'd never used one in my life. Our rifle instructor told me I had the eye for it and maybe I did, but none in the regiment could shoot like the lads from the countryside, where they were used to handling firearms.

We were soon designated our roles and I was to be a driver/wireless operator. There would be three of us to a truck and any one of us might be expected to drive or operate the wireless, as well as take care of and fire the 2 pound anti tank gun attached to our vehicle. This would involve knowing how to strip the gun down and oil it, which though a messy and intricate operation, was vital if we were to have a gun that was ready to be used at a moment's notice.

I was both astonished and pleased to learn that Ted Willis would share a truck with me; it seemed I couldn't shake off the gentle giant, but why would I want to? We were to be joined by Jimmy Kite, a much shorter fellow, but what he lacked in stature he more than made up for in strength. The stocky, athletic little man with a twinkle in his eye quickly became my closest friend and was the ideal companion to our tight knit little group. He didn't make any demands and had no ego as such, making him the perfect team player. Jimmy and I would talk to each other about our wives, although generally speaking he didn't have a great deal to say, yet when it came to the subject of Kitty Kite it was difficult to silence him. Kitty was a thin rake-like woman of great spirit, who'd lost one of her eyes in an industrial accident, yet the way Jimmy's face changed when he talked of her, it was easy to see he loved her deeply.

The next part of our training involved learning how to drive in a variety of formations and under various conditions, such as attack or retreat and I remember struggling with the instructions a wee bit when they were screamed out at us. I therefore scribbled them down on the back of a map of Liverpool and that night when were supposed to be asleep, myself and Ted and Jimmy put our heads together to figure it out and get it fixed in our minds. We sat huddled in a tent like three schoolboys, whispering to each other and looking at our combined notes by torchlight. We did this because apart from understanding how vital this could be once we were in the theatre of war, but we also knew were to be tested the very next day. The sergeant major we were allocated took no prisoners. We awoke groggy through lack of sleep, but I was all too aware I was the designated driver. I took solace in fact that we were as prepared as we could be and I can report we passed the test with flying colours, although I cannot say the same for our comrades at arms. Our fiery NCO pulled one man from his cab, after his third attempt to complete a tricky manoeuvre. It seemed that burning the midnight oil had been worth every minute of our time.

Inside our tents we were given panyas sacks to fill with straw, to sleep on, but I was usually so exhausted at the end of the day that I would have slept on a clothesline.

That night after our driver training I could have slept standing up.

4

Bullying is something that should have no place in a modern society. But as on the schoolyard, the armed forces are a place where a group of individuals come together from diverse backgrounds. This inevitably produces what is one of the worst human traits. I'd been worried something like this would happen and it had played on my mind from the day I'd taken my medical. It was then I set eyes on many of the extremely young and vulnerable young men who were to be my fellow soldiers. I kept my eyes and ears open, hoping my experience and extra years might count for something in the face of any apparent brutality.

It was at Sennybridge that I came across it for the first time as a soldier. There was a slight lad who couldn't have been more than eighteen or nineteen years old, who was a bit naive and was billeted with somebody I'd call a good time Charley and a bit of a smart Alec to boot. The lad went by the nickname Floppy and I never learned his real name, as was often the case his adopted name stuck and rather suited his relaxed demeanour. The man he was sharing a tent with, a fellow named Edgington, got the lad to fetch and carry for him and his two cronies, but the lad soon wised up to it. He might have been laid back, but he was no mug.

We were about half way through a ten mile hike, carrying a full pack plus rifle when we stopped to take on some water, a bite of bully beef and some bread, during a thirty minute rest. Our commanding officer had gone off to relieve himself when a scuffle broke out. It seemed Floppy had been unwittingly carrying some of Edgington's kit in his already heavy pack and having discovered the fact when reaching in for his own ration, emptied the items onto the ground, voicing his objection strongly. Edgington and his two shameless flunkies didn't take too well to Floppy standing up to them and threatened to work him over if he caused a fuss. I jumped to my feet and made my way to the edge of a wooded area where I found Edgington astride the young soldier, his two cronies assisting him, by pinning the lad to the ground. His bloodied nose showed that Edgington had already landed at least one cowardly blow to his face.

"What's going on here?" I asked.

"Piss off Granddad, this is none a your affair," Edgington said, spitting his words out at me, still sitting on top of the prone lad.

"And what if I make it my affair?"

He scowled and looked up at me, hoping his glare would have me shaking in my boots.

"Then you'll get some a the same. Isn't that right Sid?"

Only Sid didn't answer.

"Does thar' apply to me also?" bellowed big Ted, who'd stealthily followed me.

"An' me?" chipped in Jimmy, pushing up the sleeves of his tunic to reveal short, hairy, but extremely muscular arms.

"Who do you lot think you are, the three bleedin' musketeers?" Edgington snorted, climbing to his feet and showing some bravado. He wasn't ready to back down in front of his friends.

"Nothing like that, we were just wondering if you three big men would like to try and explain to us why you were picking on this lad?"

"It's not like tha'," Sid finally spoke up.

"Then explain it to us, we're good listeners, or perhaps you'd rather explain it to the NCO."

Edgington ground his crooked teeth and clenched his fists and made his final play. He moved forward and stood nose to nose with me, his sour breath in my face.

"This is none a your business Brown, now piss off before I put myself on charge for knockin' your block off."

"Feel free to take your best shot. They won't get involved unless your mates do and I won't go running to the brass, not as long as it's a fair fight. Or do you prefer victims who can't fight back?"

His face was scarlet, for two pins he would have laid into me, but whether it was the shadow cast across the ground by big Ted, or my apparent calmness in the face of his best bluff I'll never know.

He turned away from me and took up a sardonic pose, before he spoke again.

"You drivers can't take a joke that's all. We was only foolin' with the lad. Weren't we Floppy?" he said ruffling the lad's hair. But the blood on the much younger man's upper lip and his frightened eyes told another story, "we thought It'd be a bir' a fun to let the lad carry ar' gear for a bit that's all, didn't we boys?"

But their silence spoke volumes.

"You come with us lad. We always complete our runs with the same weight in every man's pack," big Ted barked and nobody argued.

"Oh and you can move your gear out when we get back Edgington," Jimmy added.

"What?"

"I'm movin' in with Floppy. We can swap places. I'm sure you won't mind movin' in with Tommy Collins. He'll be only too happy to carry some a your kit for yer."

"It's no skin off my nose," he answered, but his red face betrayed his true feelings. Collins was a renowned amateur boxer and although he was the perfect gentleman, there was no tougher man in the regiment.

Just then our NCO returned and stood at my shoulder.

"Everything alright here?"

"Just peachy," Edgington replied.

"Good. We move out in ten minutes."

We nodded and moved away from the trees with Floppy in tow.

*

That night as I stood on the edge of camp for my final smoke of the day, I looked up at the clear sky and thought it might be cold enough for a frost overnight. Out here in the middle of nowhere we hardly ever heard the sound of aircraft and it made me wonder, not for the first time how Anne and the children were this night. I just hoped their sky was as clear and free from enemy aircraft. It was easy to forget your other life in this regimented existence of eat, sleep and exercise. Almost every waking moment was taken up and at bedtime, my eyelids were so heavy I'd start trying to picture Anne's lovely face, but seconds later I'd be asleep.

Anne had written often, but her letters were short and to the point. She was no scholar, as she'd often say. Mother's letters were much longer and more informative, but less frequent. A little taste of homemadethe fact I was to be pitched into battle all the more like a fantasy, but the reality was soon to hit home. Our regiment was due to be shipped abroad to North Africa to fight Rommel, but first we were given seven days' leave and for me it couldn't come quick enough. I longed for the sight and sound of my close knit family. Even though our tough training regime left little time for home sickness, I was desperate for a change of scenery when the time came.

5

    My journey home took me back through endless, nameless railway stations and rain filled green fields and valleys that I was not sure I would ever see again. But I told myself that if I survived the war I'd like to see all of this as a civilian, with my family at my side. Of course I couldn't know what trials I'd need to overcome to make that a reality and in hindsight it was a good thing.

    I sat through the rest of the journey in my dress uniform, enjoying the admiring glances from children and adults alike, my body in the best condition it had ever been in.

    The train pulled into Lime Street and the station somehow seemed smaller, could it be that it had been shrunk for the war effort, or had I grown bigger? I doubted both, so I settled on the thought that my perspective had changed. I noticed the local trains had their windows blacked out, just like our homes and I was grateful this hadn't applied to our train on such a long journey. The platform was crowded, but not like it had been when I left and I saw my girl right away as the locomotive slowed. Her big eyes were even wider than I remembered, as she searched the faces on the train for sight of me. When our eyes met her face lit up like a Christmas tree and my heart soared.

    The doors were pushed open and I grabbed my things and ran to where Anne stood alone, throwing my bags down at her feet as she rushed into my arms. She smelled of perfume and baby powder and her lips were soft and tasted of lipstick and peppermint. Anne had a perpetual sweet tooth. We said nothing at first and just held each other, enjoying the feel, the look and the sweet taste of the moment.

    Eventually I gathered up my belongings and she linked me.

    "You seem thinner in the face, but stronger in the arm."

    I smiled at her and told her I felt fitter than I'd ever been in my life.

    She cuddled into my neck and whispered to me.

    "You'll need to be for whar' I've got in mind for you."

    We stopped and kissed again and it took us a moment to realise the air raid siren was sounding.

    It was no surprise as the Lufftwaffe were bombing the Port of Liverpool around the clock and as Lime Street railway station was only a couple of miles away, it wasn't the safest place to be.

    We rushed for the underground shelter without another word.

I held Anne in the grey light as we made ourselves comfortable on my luggage. The place smelled of damp and fear. Her big eyes looked in the direction of the shelter exit for any sign of the all clear, and I have to confess she was much calmer than me. I suppose it was because she'd had a lot more experience of moments like this. This after all had become part of every day life for my beautiful, brave and perky wife.

As I looked upon her serene profile, her coat opened and I was shocked to note that she'd either piled on the weight or looked to be pregnant again.

"Anne?" I said, taking her hand and pointing to her bump, "when were you planning to tell me?"

"I didn't wanna worry you. You've enough on your plate right now," she shouted back over the din.

Just then the all clear sounded and our fellow shelter dwellers stood in the gloom and made their way out. We stood there momentarily and I placed my hand to her stomach gently.

"Such a little bump," I added, "how far along are you?"

"I reckon about five months, but it's a girl this time, boys are all out front. You remember the way I was with James."

"How are the children holding up?"

"James misses you so much, but doesn't like to show it."

"Brave boy."

"Like his Father," she said quickly kissing me on the cheek and snuggling into my neck. "Emily's gor' an idea what's goin' on, but she'll know a bit more when she claps eyes on you."

"Come on let's get out of here."

But she held her ground and looked at me with a sheen in her eye I recognised.

"You know I think I fancy you more in uniform," she told me, before taking my face in her hands and kissing it passionately, she then moved closer and the second kiss was much longer. I was getting a bit hot under the collar, but grabbed her hand and pulled her away.

"Let's at least wait 'til we get home, this is a terrible place and no good for that kind of thing, especially for a woman in your condition."

She came reluctantly.

"Spoil sport," she whispered in my ear.

*

We caught the tram and huddled together behind the blacked out windows, as Anne asked me about my training and I caught up on the news from home. When we reached Harrogate Street it was close to blackout and the street was deserted, not even the local ARP warden whose job it was ensure that blackout was strictly observed was anywhere to be seen. Anne opened the door and we stumbled into the pitch-black room, unable to see a hand in front of either of our faces.

In an instant a shout went up and gas lamps were quickly lit, to reveal my parents, Peter and Elsie, William Groves, my sister Margie who was now twenty. She was standing with a young man I didn't know, flanking my two children. Emily was rubbing her eyes as she smiled shyly at a man she barely recognised and hadn't seen very much of recently. I took her in my arms and gave her a squeeze. I then dropped to my knees and kissed my son, who as Anne had predicted was putting on a brave face, but quickly put his arms about me and started to waffle on about a tin soldier he held in his tiny hand.

Successfully reacquainted with my children, somebody pressed a bottle of Guinness and a glass into my hand and I rounded on my guests. Emily smiling across at me in Anne's arms - James holding onto my trousers for dear life.

"To Angus," my Mother said, raising a glass, "may he make us all proud and return in one piece."

Everyone drank to this and much later my Father sidled up to me and added quietly and out of earshot to my Mother,

"We're already proud of you son. Just come back to us, that's all we want," he told me, as the incessant water works started again and he nearly had me crying with him, on my first night home in nearly two months.

Margie who was now an extremely attractive, buxom young woman, eagerly introduced me to Albert Smedley who I took to right away. He worked at the butchers next door to *Taylor's* where Margie worked as a shop assistant and they met when she brought him his morning paper each day. Albert, not a man to look a gift horse in the mouth, quickly realised what a remarkable woman my sister is and asked her out. They soon became inseparable and would be the same for decades to come, and I must add that nobody on God's earth could dislike Albert, he was one of life's gentlemen and genuine to the core. He and I got on famously from that point onward.

Mother updated me on Johnny's exploits in the RAF and explained he was based in Scotland. He was doing well and sent his love. Peter announced he'd applied to join the Royal Artillery too, having finally received his call up papers. I told him that I wouldn't object, on the sole condition he didn't mention I was his brother. He laughed hard and the bond that had always existed between us was as strong as it had ever been.

The children were both asleep in the same bed by the time the party started to wind down and I think it was my yawning that eventually drove everybody away. It had been a long and exciting day and in all honesty for these past weeks it was way past my bedtime. In fact, true to form I was asleep before Anne had crept in beside me and if she was disappointed she didn't say.

6

As early as 1939 children had been evacuated to what were considered to be safe rural areas. The children from Liverpool mostly journeyed to Lancashire and North Wales. In those days when people seldom travelled, a journey to the likes of Skelmersdale, only about ten miles away; was considered a long journey. The elderly and childless were paid a sum in line with the Anderson Committee for taking evacuees in. They collected their payment from a local Post Office, a bit like collecting family allowance in those days. This was not considered to be compulsory according to our Government, but word was that people were threatened with fines if they were recognised as suitable, yet refused to comply.

Anne rejected the idea throughout 1939 and right up until 1942, taking the view that she wanted her children with her, and insisting most vehemently that she was the only person who would look after them properly. Now Anne's views cannot be considered without knowing her background and although I wanted my children safe and ideally evacuated, I was in no position to argue. Anne eventually conceded she might consider evacuating if there was no other option, but only if she could accompany them.

We left it at that.

Meanwhile our friend Hitler, having declared a blockade of Britain, was bombing London, Southampton, Bristol, Cardiff, Manchester and Liverpool, where he hoped to cut our supply lines.

Two other interesting facts that would shape the war occurred in September, one was US conscription and the other, the signing of the Tripartite Axis pact, by Germany, Italy and Japan. There was also the re-election of Roosevelt as US president during November of 1940, a man who was warming to the endeavours of Britain and what remained of her allies. The war in Africa was also hotting up, in readiness for my arrival, as Britain began a western desert offensive against the occupying Italians during early December.

*

I tried to squeeze every drop of enjoyment from my time at home, treating my leave a bit like a holiday. The children had never had a more attentive Father and Anne couldn't get rid of me during the day and remonstrated with me, claiming my constant gawping at her was preventing her from doing her housework properly. I assume she was relieved therefore when I was dragged off to the pub in the evenings by numerous members of our combined family. There were stacks of unread magazines and papers and Anne was a little puzzled when I continued to ignore them.

"There'll be plenty of time for reading Anne. But not now when time seems so precious. I just can't be bothered with it in all honesty. I'll take most of it with me for the journey," I remember saying and bizarrely for somebody who could hardly keep his nose out of a book or magazine, I found it impossible to concentrate on the printed word.

Yet mentioning the inevitable wasn't clever, Anne who would have had me doing almost anything to avoid the call up was still touchy about the subject. Many local men had joined the Fire Brigade and other services such as the ARP (Air Raid Protection) wardens and LDV (Local Defence Volunteers) in an effort to delay or prevent their call up. I'd made it clear to Anne I would not be following suit and I don't think she ever understood why, no matter how hard I tried to explain my ideology to her. To her it was simply about survival, but to me it was living with myself if I somehow shirked my responsibility. No, for me, my only concession was waiting for the call up.

We tried to make our last day and night as normal as possible and though we'd tried to avoid watching the clock the day eventually ebbed away and we found ourselves sharing a bed, never knowing whether we would ever do so again.

She asked if I'd any ideas about a name for the new baby. I reached across and rested my hand onto her stomach gently and said,

"If you're so sure it's a girl, how about Rhona?"

"I like it, but wherever did you come up with such a name?"

"Our Commanding Officer is a very decent fellow and that's his daughter's name and he absolutely dotes on her. In fact she's all he talks about. I liked the name when I first heard it and to be honest we've about used up the female family names on her Royal Highness Emily Frances Brown."

Anne laughed at this and said,

"She is ar' little Princess so it's only proper," she said giggling again and it was good to her really laugh. It had seemed an awfully long time since I'd heard Anne's laughter and I found that thought sobering. This was another thing Mr Hitler had stolen from us.

"What if it's a boy?" I asked.

"It won't be," she assured me. "Rhona she will be."

7

This time I said my goodbyes to most of my family at home and Anne and I made our way to the Pier Head by tram, leaving behind everything that was most dear to us in the world.

It was much harder than the emotionally charged parting at Lime Street a couple of months before. This time I was entering the unknown and I had to face up to the fact that I might return in a wooden box. It was the real thing this time, no dress rehearsal and I could very well pay for my ideology with my life. I'd already been forced to face up to this when filling in my last will and testament on page 15 of my Soldiers Service book. I didn't dare mention any of this to Anne and therefore ensured that this particular document was carefully hidden, in the deluge of reading material stored at the bottom of my kit bag.

I'd been inoculated against cholera, another thing I kept to myself, but there was no injection that would make me bullet proof.

We found our way to the troop ship that had once been a luxury liner in peace time and we held onto each other until the very last moment. It was chaotic, as we were surrounded by thousands of uniformed personnel and their girls and wives in the same situation.

The final call came and I was ordered aboard. I made my way with a heavy heart and a feeling of utter hopelessness, as though I was part of a huge herd of cattle on our way to the abattoir. So much so that I felt like I'd been anaesthetised, as I was jostled along the gangplank, lost in a sea of uniformed men.

Once more the situation I found myself in just didn't seem real.

I furiously waved to Anne from the rail of the ship as did hundreds of my fellow conscripts. Whether she'd been able to pick me out I didn't know, yet I watched and waved on helplessly as we slowly made our way out into Liverpool Bay. I stood in the same spot straining my eyes until Anne was no more than an unrecognisable speck in the distance.

I stumbled across Ted and Jimmy Kite and Floppy found us.

As a regiment and a fighting force, we were a mass of pent up emotion and a glut of coarse humour and what I can only describe as high jinks took place. But there was nothing too serious, harmless pranks mostly, although one or two men found themselves confined to their bunks for lengthy spells. In reality it was nothing more than a group of nervous young men facing up to their responsibilities and letting off a little steam in the process.

The ship anchored, still within sight of Liverpool Docks, to wait for a convoy to lead us to foreign waters. I'd often stand at the rail of this former liner and gaze at the City. So near yet so far and she'd never looked more lovely to me, with the pre- blackout lights reflecting on the Mersey in the fading light. Then against the skyline, I could see the architecture that truly sets Liverpool apart from any other place. I'm talking about those two fictitious birds perched atop the Liver building watching over our people. A sight that for some reason spoke of defiance to me that day and I remember thinking that as long as they stayed in place, Liverpool would survive.

Our stationary situation precipitated a period of never-ending lifeboat drills, card games and private contemplation. There was also the unknown, as we were unaware of our exact destination. Also at about that time we were issued with tropical kit and every man was given 2 mepracine tablets to protect us against malaria.

At last there was a flurry of activity and we joined a convoy of ships that would hopefully lead us safely through the war-ravaged Atlantic Ocean. Men were sick by the dozens, but I was spared from the indignation of sea sickness. It became even worse for some men as we journeyed through the Bay of Biscay, an area notorious for rough seas in autumn and winter. It was so bad that the toilets permanently smelled of vomit.

I remember that Floppy was a sufferer and although big Ted was not sick it was clear that he didn't have sea legs. It was therefore left to me and Jimmy to look after the lad and we did what we could, buying buns for him from the NAAFI shop as he was unable to tolerate the ration of fatty pork we were issued at meal times.

Finally we reached our destination, which was Algiers and were ushered aboard landing craft, known as LCPs, in full kit. When we landed we were forced to dig in after we were greeted by a barrage of enemy shells and I remember thinking that they could have given us a little time to settle on land, but thinking logically I realised they knew exactly what they were doing. I kept my head down and my eyes open as our equipment and trucks were unloaded in the worst possible circumstances.

8

The war in North Africa was strategically important for a number of reasons. Our main motivation was the Suez Canal and tied into this, our efforts to keep the Allied supply lines open. Another was that this particular war acted at something of a distraction to dear old Mr Hitler, preventing him from diverting his resources to the Russian problem that was becoming something of a nuisance to him.

I didn't realise it at the time, but I was joining the only true land battle of the war, which we would take to the Germans from 1940 through to September of 1943. I was also ignorant to the fact that when my tour began we were vastly outnumbered and inferior in terms of armoury and weaponry. It was a crude awakening for me, when I was astonished to discover that our 2 pound anti tank guns were virtually useless against their Tiger and Panzer tanks. It wasn't until we'd captured a few of those tanks that we were to learn they featured double armour plating and not only that, but their weaponry had so much more power than ours. Our six-pound guns were a little more effective, yet still no match for the German armoury. Our Matilda and Grant tanks were also impotent when compared to the German equivalents and early in the conflict our losses were about 8 times heavier than theirs.

But, like us they still had to deal with the elements. The baking heat of day was a factor, as were the freezing conditions overnight and the sudden changes in the weather that were often followed by a sandstorm. In addition to this, radio transmissions were sometimes overheard by the enemy and this made it almost impossible to mount a surprise attack.

The only positives we could claim were that our war was fought with the utmost good grace. Either side would send in a medic if a man was wounded and each side observed periods of truce from time to time, in order to let the other side claim their dead and wounded. The officers leading both sets of troops were gentlemen and duly acted so.

Our vehicles were supposed to be manned by three men, all of whom shared the driving, although I have to say I did most of it. As we were trained to do, we drove in strict convoy to each destination. Partly because our NCO was a fine man, who was prepared to ignore some regulations for the good of morale, Floppy always rode with us and because he was significantly taller than me, I often drove sitting on his knee. That was made easy as the gearshift was on the steering wheel.

Quite early on in the conflict, our cook who'd been specially trained to feed the men on what he could lay his hands on, was killed in action and yours truly was one of three men given the dubious honour of pitching in.

Making camp was nearly always a hurried affair, but we were expected to dig ourselves holes in record time, dig latrines and each take a turn standing watch. We could be in the same place for days and sometimes weeks and along with the enemy, we did battle with rats, horse flies, gnats, giant spiders, the occasional scorpion and a number of dangerous snakes.

As we made camp one particular evening it was my turn to take first watch. Night fell quickly and I took my heavy army coat to ward off the cold, armed with my Enfield rifle, a torch and a dog-eared J B Priestley novel. The first hour passed peacefully enough, but as the second began, I heard footsteps come up behind me and turned swiftly but silently, pointing my rifle and torch into the darkness, in a sweeping motion.

A voice spoke from the blackness,

"Don't shoot Gus. It's only me."

Floppy walked into the dim light of my torch.

"Good God lad I almost shot you. What are you doing creeping about like that?" I asked him, keeping the fact that my hands were trembling to myself.

"Sorry but I couldn't sleep. Cigarette?"

He smiled at me and I took one of the offered smokes before ruffling his hair. We sat in silence for a while, but when he spoke his voice was thick with emotion.

"This is nothing like I expected. It's difficult to put into words what I imagined it might be like, but all I know is that it was nothing like this. I was hoping I'd feel proud to serve," he told me, then stopped and took control of his emotions. It was then I realised how hard it must have been for him to open up to me in this way. After a few more puffs on his smoke he spoke again. "I've come to the conclusion that War is a filthy thing Gus and I wish I was at home, where all I had to worry about was bombs dropping overhead and getting to the shelter in one piece."

"Look son we all feel the same way. We're men doing what's expected of us at times like this. Nobody here is enjoying himself. We've just got to help each get through it."

"We're not all men."

I said nothing, but instead turned to see him cover his eyes with his left hand and begin to sob violently. I'm not normally that perceptive but I got it right away and instantly saw him for what he was.

"How old were you when you enlisted son?"

"Nearly fifteen."

He was very big for his age and mature in a lot of ways, but he was still a boy nonetheless.

"You should come clean with the top brass. They'll probably send you home. You shouldn't be here son."

"You won't tell them will you Gus?"

I remember sighing heavily, and stupidly promising I wouldn't tell anyone. Much later I stumbled into my tent and found sleep with a heavy heart, wishing I'd had the courage to turn him in, a child who'd joined up with a cockeyed view of War, a view that only an idealistic boy might have.

9

    I kept his secret close to my chest and I suppose I became more protective of him than ever, but not in a way that anyone would notice. Anne would have laughed to learn that I'd taken on the role of temporary cook for the men, but certainly wouldn't have objected to the extra pay it brought. I had no training and had certainly never cooked at home, but these were simple meals mainly consisting of stews and I can say that anything I could lay my hands on were thrown into the pot, seasoned with as much salt as I could get hold of. Each night as I made the stew my mind always returned to the boy who'd joined up to fight a man's war.

    The skin on my forearms, face and neck was now a deep mahogany and I was beginning to look like one of the locals. My lips had started to split and on top of this, the damned sand got everywhere, in our boots, undergarments and even the food. Anne's quick fire letters were gratefully received along with the occasional lengthier letter from my Mother. It seemed that Anne's intuition had been correct and our third child was born a girl and she was given the name Rhona as we'd agreed. My Mother wrote and explained what a bonny child she was; yet she seemed sickly and although Anne fretted over her, she didn't like to burden me and I raised my eyes to heaven. I was used to this from Anne and was helpless to influence her in anyway, stuck in the middle of nowhere surrounded by sand and the African Corps.

    We were often aided by various Australian and New Zealand forces from time to time and their help was always welcome, but the men who had the most profound effect on me were the Ghurkhas.

    I befriended a man I only knew as Lan, who told me he was a Naik (Corporal), explaining he had ten riflemen under his control. He had a coal black face, but a set of perfect pearl white teeth. He was a soft spoken man and I had to strain to hear him, but his English was perfect and he explained that he and his family had learned it to gain work. He furthermore explained that the proud Ghurkhas of Nepal fought a series of bloody wars against the British Army, but when a truce was agreed around 1816 the two factions retained the utmost respect for each other. Men started to join an army run by the East India Railway Company and what began as an affinity with the British eventually developed into the formation of seven Ghurkha regiments in the British army. They carried army issue rifles, but he and his comrades also carried a long, curved, fierce looking knife (known as a khurkuri), that Lan assured me, matter of factly, was sharp enough to sever a man's head.

I didn't doubt it.

One incident in particular underlined the effectiveness of those proud warriors, who were only with us in an effort to gain safe passage through the battle zone. They were true warriors and the Allies intended to use them in situations when hand to hand combat was a probability. And the events about to unfold proved to me that these unassuming men were being deployed precisely in the right way.

*

We were involved in a heavy exchange of artillery with a German Division we'd quite literally stumbled across. Although we had the element of surprise on our side the Germans were superior in numbers and firepower. After hours of gruelling battle we were forced to retreat to a position that left us open to a classic pincer attack and before we knew it, our regiment was completely surrounded. Before darkness fell, a truce was arranged to allow each side to gather up the dead and injured and I recall a courteous German Doctor offering his services. I also remember thinking that Mr Hitler would have been astonished by the man's offer of assistance, not to mention his swarthy skin and dark brown eyes. This man was hardly of Hitler's beloved Aryan race.

Nevertheless it was an offer we graciously refused.

Our Ghurka comrades were another group of men Herr Hitler would not have approved of, and even though they'd unwittingly stumbled into a hopeless situation, Lan and his company gave the impression the events unfolding were completely natural. To a man, they showed no sign of nerves.

Night fell like a huge blackout blanket and although it was highly unusual for either side to launch an attack under cover of darkness, no man slept soundly. We were entirely surrounded as I've said and no man expected to be free the following day, if he was lucky enough to survive the obvious early assault that was expected to render us helpless.

It was nothing like we expected.

When daylight reared its head, a strange atmosphere met each waking man, as our commanding officers roused us. They knew what had occurred of course. The Ghurkhas had ventured into the night with their long knives and slaughtered the Germans surrounding us.

They simply hadn't stood a chance.

We made our way through a swathe of dead bodies and as you do in such circumstances, thanked the Gods that we were still alive. It's an awful thing to admit but once a man has grown accustomed to the sight and smell of death, he is truly grateful to be alive and I'm not ashamed to say that this is exactly how I felt.

10

It was soon May of 1942 and I'd been in North Africa for fourteen months when our Commanding Officer announced we were due for five days' leave and I can tell you I was looking forward to some well-earned respite. We'd earned the occasional day or so of leave that had ended in a drunken stupor for most, plus a visit to the fleshpots of the area, plying their trade on the Allied side of the fence, but despite my usual proclivity for alcohol I somehow couldn't let my guard down completely. Even a man on leave should be ready to be recalled at any moment, I told myself, and I could understand now why the giraffe sleeps with one eye open. In the theatre of war, not one man from our company could claim to have been soundly asleep on any given night and it was a hard habit to break.

History now shows we were losing the war in the desert during the early part of 1942 and it was during a battle in early June at Knightsbridge, near Tobruk when this became all too clear to me.

We'd advanced on a German patrol and held our position overnight, expecting to launch a surprise attack and as I wasn't on watch I made for my tent and fell into a deep, troubled sleep. I dreamt that Anne and the children had been captured by faceless henchmen and as dreams of that type tend to be, no matter how hard I tried I couldn't save them, they were constantly at arm's length from me.

I awoke in a cold sweat just after dawn and as I knew I wouldn't find sleep again anytime soon, I relieved Jimmy who was on watch but fast asleep. He staggered to his billet as I watched the sun slowly come up from behind the sand dunes and within a couple of hours we were assembled in full battle dress and ready to go.

Ted and Jimmy were to my left as I perched myself on Floppy's knee and pushed my vehicle forward, but to our horror it seemed that we'd been outflanked by the African Corps, who were massed in significant number close by.

We did what we could, but for every shell we fired, their tanks kept coming protected by that damned double armour plating. Our only hope was a hit and run strategy, as we were vastly outnumbered and couldn't compete with their defences or firepower.

Suddenly a barrage of shells rained down upon our troops and we suffered heavy casualties. The noise rang in my ears as one minute we manned our guns, the next we retreated. The din from explosions was all about us and it was like being in the centre of some horrendous dream. There seemed no escape from the noise and death crashing down on us from the clear sky above. It was relentless and unforgiving.

When it happened it seemed to be in slow motion. The four of us were in the cab and I remember closing my eyes and ducking as a shell landed too close for comfort. Shrapnel from the blast peppered the truck and I dashed out into the smoke and smell of cordite, turning to urge the others to join me. It was then I realised Jimmy had been hit. I couldn't see big Ted, but my eyes strayed to the left of the cab to where the lad's prone shape had taken the full force of the shrapnel, high up on the chest. He was dead without question, a boy who should have been at home with his Mother.

I looked on in horror as the guilt began to form, quickly followed by a searing heat that seemed to burn my skull. I started to lose consciousness, eventually sliding uncontrollably into the blackness that suddenly swamped me.

I had also been hit.

Anne with James, Emily and baby Rhona

Anne's Story - part 3

1

I dropped onto the hard kitchen chair like a stone, but felt nothing. Every part of my being was in shock.

I stared across at the telegram on the kitchen table and the torn envelope, just to make sure they were real. I could hear Emily and Jim playing together happily, but I was I was in a deep, dark place and even though my eyes were open, I could see nothing but darkness and despair brought about by that dreaded piece of paper.

*

I made my way back home after seeing Angus to his ship. I was cold, hungry and parched, having hung around much longer than I intended to. Emily had taken the children for the night and I was grateful for it. I was exhausted and my mood was black. But as far I'm concerned it was allowed, after all; it's not every day a girl sees her man off to war. I took a long soak in the bath in front of the fire, expecting no visitors and it was only as I was dressing upstairs that I heard a tap at the window. I made my way down and opened the front door to find Groves and ar' Tommy standing in front of me grinning inanely, obviously the worse for drink. They'd called 'round with beer and a box of Swiss chocolates that Tommy threw into my lap. I picked them up and gave Tommy one of my looks.

"Wherever did you get these?"

"Now thar'd be tellin' Anne," he answered, grinning again.

"Well come 'ere then and give me an 'ug."

We embraced and I soon established he was on leave for ten days, after which he was due to be shipped off to the North Atlantic with the Royal Navy.

He was still in uniform and I have to say that even though I detested all of them, it rather suited him, the dark blue working well with his jet black hair and pale complexion.

"We thought you probably needed a little cheerin' up," he said opening a bottle of beer and handing it to me.

We sat and I put the wireless on low.

Soon we were chatting, happily regaled by Tommy's basic training adventures. He did have a way of telling a story that made you feel as though you'd actually been there. He could paint a little picture with his words and actions and soon I began to feel better, allowing Groves' deep, soothing voice to wash over me and Tommy's insatiable appetite for life to bring me back to life.

Realising that Angus would not be able to get news of the war I began to scour the newspapers when the children were in bed and tried to pick out any positives. I sent him a weekly letter and included snippets about the children along with a war update, but after telling him how much I loved him, there didn't seem much else to say. For example I told him about the Yugoslav's overthrowing the pro axis government in March of 1941, but didn't mention their surrender in late July. I didn't tell him that the *Bismark* had sunk the British ship *Hood* in May of 1941, but made a point of letting him know that the British Navy had sunk the *Bismark* later that month. I didn't care to mention that the word on the street was we were losing the war. Propaganda in the newspapers and on the wireless meant that they didn't tell us the truth and I may be many things, but naïve isn't one of them. I understood why as a people we had to maintain hope and also knew that the men fighting for our cause could not know what the man on the street feared.

2

During March and April, my mother-in-law - aided and abetted by old Groves - urged me to have the children evacuated, fearing the mass bombing that was rumoured to be coming our way. We knew well enough that after London we were probably the next target of the Luftwaffe.

But as it has already been documented, I was a stubborn cow and I would not send my children away, unless I was prepared to go with them. I can't explain it any other way; other than to say that I wanted to be here for him when he came home and it seemed wrong to me somehow, abandoning him, but I was almost made to regret it during the so-called blitz of May 1941.

This was when Hitler attempted to tear the heart out of Liverpool, with over 500 air raids and a total of 79 bombs dropped on our city for 8 consecutive days. During this time, 870 tonnes of high explosive bombs and over 112,000 firebombs were dropped in a relentless attempt to level the city and bring us to our knees. Each night, shortly after midnight, the Luftwaffe pounded our helpless city and surrounding areas with bombs, parachute mines and incendiary devices.

In all, 1,746 people lost their lives and 1,154 were seriously injured, resulting in a mass funeral at Anfield cemetery on 14 May, when around 1,000 people were buried in a common grave. From those of us who survived, over 50,000 people were made homeless, but such was the determination of Liverpudlians to ensure the Germans wouldn't win, the authorities somehow found these people homes, although some were forced to move out of Liverpool and into surrounding districts. On top of this, many of the seriously injured were moved out of the city to be cared for because the hospitals and morgues were completely full.

As it was happening, the propaganda machine prevented the rest of the country from knowing the full extent of the devastation and loss of life. We were merely referred to as 'the northern city' who were suffering. How we survived it I'll never know, but the unflagging pride and sense of humour of all Liverpudlians must have played a big part.

When the 8 days passed, the Germans transferred their formidable military powers to the Russian front and although there were still air raids to follow, there was nothing on the scale of the May blitz anywhere in the entire country.

Churchill himself commented on the Liverpool Blitz, saying;
'I see the damage done by the enemy attacks, but I also see the spirit of an unconquered people.'

I knew Angus would like that and I remember writing it down for him word for word. I, of course failed to record the true scale of what had occurred, continually using my own particular brand of propaganda.

After The Blitz I was able to sleep in my own bed most nights, but every now and again I'd drift into sleep and awaken, believing momentarily he was beside me. I'd swear I could see the outline of his body through half opened eyes and of course I'd soon come to my senses and find I was alone in our big empty bed again. At such times, my body, in fact my entire being, ached for him and I'd lie awake trying to picture his face, or the touch of his slender hands. The long fingers and the hairs on the back of his hands that were as soft as the finest silk would come to my mind easily for some reason. Yet I could only snatch at the slightest hint of his fabulous smile, why was that?

Some nights I'd open our wardrobe and take hold of a sleeve from one of his jackets and lift it to my face, to drink in any trace of the scent of my man. It would do no good at all, but at this point I was well beyond rational thought, my emotions had completely taken over and I went with them in wild abandonment.

3

I've heard it said and have often read that men and women experience different sexual urges and I suppose in my experience that has more than a ring of truth. The War placed many respectable married women in a totally abnormal situation. Those of us who were happily married had mostly been used to a healthy physical and emotional relationship with our men. Yet even some women in that same category succumbed to a condition that afflicted people of every sexual persuasion throughout Britain. Perhaps because of the closeness of our communities, the tongues would wag when a neighbour you'd known for years would suddenly be seen on the arm of a stranger. I tried very hard not to judge any of them and instead tried to understand why they did it. Too many of my neighbours were only too ready to ostracise such women when what some of them needed was our help and sympathy. I'd begun to recognise and even share the emotions that drove them into the arms of men who'd somehow avoided the draft, but my sympathies ended when I considered the men who preyed on the fear and hopelessness we all endured. Some, I'm sure, just wanted something to distract them and block out the dread and anxiety that had become a part of everyday life. Others, I believe, needed a shoulder to lean on and if it meant giving up a few sexual favours in return for a little strength, I suppose they considered this a reasonable trade off.

Some, of course, ended up with another mouth to feed for their indiscretions. These women I pitied the most. Some took their own lives, others took the babies' lives. Some simply went away and did not return. Many marriages were over when the war ended because of this, but equally some survived. In my own mind I could only conclude that women who strayed could never have experienced what Angus and I had, but deep down I knew there was more to it. Personality and life experience also had to be added into the mix to get a true picture.

I'd like to say I was stronger than these women, but I think I was just lucky to have a man worth waiting for and perhaps my own life experiences influenced my thinking. Angus and I had created a family and I was determined my children would know both of their parents if the war was to last ten years, because I knew only too clearly what the alternative was.

I prefer to think of myself as one of the lucky ones and I was not alone. There were many thousands of women like me who held onto their virtue and waited and hoped beyond hope our men would make it through.

During the summer of 1941 there was no doubt in anybody's mind that Churchill was beginning to influence Roosevelt as the Americans slowly became embroiled in the conflict. In July of 1941 the American President took the decision to freeze Japanese assets in the States, and at the same time, suspended relations with the country for their aggression against neighbouring nations.

Gradually, they became inextricably involved, and I suspect a cunning, cigar smoking Prime Minister of ours was extremely influential regarding their gradual shift in stance. I think he realised that if the Americans were involved there would only be one winner of this war.

On 7th December of 1941, as history will show, the Japanese bombed Pearl Harbour and by the following day Britain and America had jointly declared war on the Japanese. And, by the 11th, of December, Churchill got the Christmas present I believe he most wanted, when Germany declared war on America.

I hoped this would hasten the end of the conflict, but the devastating news I was to receive in the form of a telegraph tore my heart open and sent my dreams and desires spinning violently out of control.

4

I'd never received a telegram before and I must tell you my legs buckled when the messenger rapped heavily on my door and I realised why this nondescript man was standing before me. His face was stoic and I suppose it was the same everywhere for him, he was only doing his job. He was, after all, as disconnected from this entire transaction as the paper and ink, so why should any of it mean a thing to him?

I took the packet from him and I think I muttered something like thanks, but the words were jammed in my windpipe and I looked down at the buff envelope as though it was about to bite me.

*

I don't know how long I stood in the narrow doorway, but the messenger had long since departed and I suddenly heard Emily's voice and saw her pretty little face looking up at me through a mist of despair.

"What's wrong mummy?" my almost three year old asked and her words jolted me out of my flux. What did it was her crumpled expression. It was clear the torment I was experiencing had registered.

"Nothin' love," I mumbled, "Mummy's just thinkin' about somethin' sad. You go and play nice now, there's a good girl." I said finally, and perhaps because of my apparent return to normality, she did.

I dropped into a chair and stared down at the still unread telegram, the panic now welling up inside of me. I almost choked on bile forming at the back of my throat and I was light headed, so much so that it seemed it might just lift right off my shoulders and float around the room.

I shut my eyes and brought my hands, that smelled faintly of bleach, up to my face.

'Oh my God, oh my God, please no, not this,' my mind screamed inside my head.

'Oh just open the bloody thing and get it over with,' it went on.

Trance-like I reached for the envelope and tore it open. It was a standard document that had been manipulated by the clerk whose terrible job it was to issue such notices. On the top right hand corner was the date of issue and address of the issuing office which was;

 R. A - for Royal Artillery - (Light AA) 2 July 1942, Ibex House, Minories, EC3.

I forced my eyes down onto the page as a vortex of emotions engulfed me again. It read;

 Dear Sir or Madam (Sir or, had been crossed through in blue ink)

 I regret to inform you that a report has been received from the War Office to the effect that (No.) 1609371 (Rank) Gunner

 (Name) BROWN Angus Mckenzie

 (Regiment) 169/57th Light AA Regiment R.A.

 was posted " MISSING " on 6 - 6 - 42.

 The report that he is missing does not necessarily mean that he has been killed, as he may have been taken prisoner of war or temporarily separated from his regiment.

 Official reports that men are prisoners of war take some time to reach this country, and if he has been captured by the enemy it is probable that unofficial news will reach you first. In that case I am to ask you to forward any postcard or letter received at once to this office, and it will be returned to you as soon as possible.

 Should any further official information be received it will be at once communicated to you.

 I am Madam your obedient servant.

 Signed P I Smith (At least that's what the signature looked like.)

 Captain of LAA RA records

 I was suddenly delirious with excitement. This was better news than I allowed myself to hope. He was 'missing' not 'killed in action'. I realised it didn't mean he was alive, but it did mean there was hope.

 I poured over the letter time after time as if the standard printed material contained some other hint about his situation I might have missed. But alas, after more than a dozen re-reads it told me no more than I'd gleaned from the first white knuckle ride of a read.

 I'd lost all track of time in my hunger to learn my husband's fate, until James tugged at my floral apron.

 "When is it tea time Mummy? I'm 'ungry."

"'ungry are yer son?" I smiled back at him, a smile that must have had a look of insanity about it.

I jumped to my feet, making him flinch, plucked him from the ground and held his little face close to mine.

"What would you like? I'll make your favourite - cheese and onion - if you like?" I then commenced to twirl him around.

"Me too mummy, pick me up as well," Emily piped up, holding her little chubby arms out to me.

I did as she asked and we all danced around and around, all giggling and laughing as we spun quicker and quicker.

Shortly afterwards, I gave my smiling and breathless children each a piece of doughy bread I'd freshly baked that day, as I grated cheese and sliced onions and although there was a smile on my face, the tears streaming from my eyes were in no way associated with the onion.

*

After we'd eaten our fill I tidied the children up and made myself presentable, then we made the short walk to James and Emily's home. On the way I was hoping Groves might be about on such an agreeable summer evening, but as he wasn't, I knew I owed it to Angus's parents and rushed in the direction of Rishton Street to bring them my news first. Emily and James took heed of their Mother and held onto the pram containing the oblivious bundle we'd named Rhona.

Emily opened the door and didn't show any surprise at my unplanned visit as I put the brake on the pram and took the baby into my arms. We all trundled inside and the children removed their coats and began to play. Rhona had no choice other than to stay with me as I delivered my news. All the time this was going on, my mother-in-law went through the process of making us tea. James was tearful, but Emily, true to form, was strong enough for all of us, as my own eyes could not hide my emotions.

5

I made my mind up very quickly. Once I'd recovered from the initial shock I came to the conclusion that me and the children must survive at any cost. I was forced to face up the fact that Angus could be buried in some unknown grave - even though I prayed he was lying injured somewhere, or had been captured by the enemy. With bombs still dropping regularly there was a possibility our luck would one day run out. I didn't dare to imagine what would become of my children if Angus was gone and I was also taken from them. I knew only too well there wasn't a William Groves in every Liverpool street and whilst he plus Emily and James would surely take my orphans in, none of them were getting any younger.

I contacted the authorities and told them that I wanted to be evacuated with them. Explaining I could keep house to pay my way, I fully expected to follow my neighbours children into North Wales, assuming from my limited knowledge that that was where they sent all evacuees.

William took the news Angus was 'missing in action' badly. He was very fond of Angus and I could see it hurt him to consider one of the very few men he was truly close to might be gone for good.

I delivered another bombshell by declaring we'd applied to be evacuated and for the very first time I watched tears well up in his eyes.

I suddenly realised that in my haste to do what I thought was right for the kids, I'd hurt him deeply. I'd cast aside the only man I thought of as my true Father and hadn't even considered asking his opinion, before plunging headlong into my decision.

"Oh Father," I said to him, "an' I meant to say that. You are my Father, my true Father. May God forgive me?"

"For what lass?" he asked, pretending not to catch my meaning.

"You know what. I've just blundered on like I always do, thinkin' I'd worked out the answer to ir all. But I 'adn't even thought about you. And I don't want you to be left 'ere all alone. Come with us?"

He smiled and touched my cheek.

"It's a lovely idea Anne, but there's my job and our homes. They'd be looted in a week and that'd be no good for anyone. Don't worry about me my girl, besides, Jock Brown and I have become quite thick these past years, I won't lack company."

He was being brave of course, but I knew there was no persuading him.

*

Our papers came through much quicker than I expected, but then again the majority of children had already been evacuated. We were to go to a place called Bryn, part of the larger district of Hindley in Wigan, a location I knew absolutely nothing about. I'd heard they talked with a strong Lancashire accent in Wigan, but were working people just like us. We were to stay with a widow, by the name of Mrs Lea.

I just hoped she'd accept us willingly. It was probably only an old wives' tales, but I'd heard that some people were not too keen on taking children into their homes, despite the financial reward paid to them by the Government. I'd also been told by one of the many gossip-mongers around and about that children were beaten and given only bread and water to eat.

As it turned out, I had nothing to worry about.

6

The weeks rushed by and the day of our departure arrived all too soon.

I'd packed everything I could carry, making sure the children had enough clothing. Yet, I found that - as the days began to diminish - I grew increasingly sentimental about the many things I'd taken for granted. Even the street itself seemed to take on a more attractive look. I found myself staring longingly at the row of terraced houses and blackout curtains that seemed to look back at me urging me to stay and just watching children from the street playing together, skipping or playing ball, I somehow found greatly moving. A great lump of emotion seemed stuck in my chest and it was as though a river of tears had become lodged in my breast.

Yet the weight of this thing I lived and breathed with, was both a blessing and a burden.

As the crow flies, Wigan is not a great distance from Liverpool, but in those days the journey was long winded. We were to take the tram to Lime Street railway station, then board a train to Wigan, only to reach our final destination by bus. It was to be a long and arduous trip with three children, but I kept telling myself I was doing the right thing.

When the day finally came for us to leave, our dwindling family consisted of Emily, James, Groves and Margie. Johnny, Peter and Tommy were all enlisted men of course and knew nothing of the plight facing Angus, but I was certain they had plenty to occupy them. Everyone insisted upon coming to Lime Street with us despite my protests on the grounds that the station was one of the more obvious targets for bombings.

Even Emily was close to tears when, I suppose, it dawned on her she could not know how long it would be before she'd see her grandchildren again. I assume she wondered whether she'd actually ever see any of us again. Who knew how long the war would last? James and Emily knew we were going on an adventure, I'd prepared them for that much and they knew we'd be living elsewhere, but when they twigged that both that of their Grandads and their Nana would not be joining us, they were inconsolable. Rhona just smiled at everyone, ignorant to the ceremony that was unfolding before her.

We all hugged and dabbed at our eyes and with a heavy heart, the river of tears I'd stored up in my chest burst its banks unexpectedly, as we boarded our train. For a good thirty minutes into the journey, I cried non-stop, ending up with a red nose and a selection of very damp handkerchiefs.

James and Emily soon recovered their composure as children do and were soon lost in games of make believe. As I watched them totally immersed in pretence I was almost jealous, what I would have given to be able to suspend reality for just a few minutes. But in another way I was happy to see my children playing as they should, in spite of the war.

I turned my troubled mind to what might await us in the alien environment that was Bryn. How would we be received?

It would be odd for the modern traveller to think of Wigan from Liverpool as a distant land when it is less than thirty miles away. Yet we were unused to travelling outside our communities in those days, never mind our towns or cities. Even the next town or village might be considered unfamiliar in.

The children were asleep when we entered the final leg of our journey and I gazed out at the green fields as the bus trundled along, with my hands clasped together in a silent prayer. The prayer went something like, 'Please God let everything turn out right for Angus, and if there's any room left, let Wigan be alright for us.'

I couldn't be further from a religious zealot, but somebody was smiling on me that day and some might say not before time.

7

Dusk was falling as the bus trundled to our destination. In truth it was more like a taxi as we were the only passengers and the driver made it plain he intended to take us directly to Mrs Lea's home. It was comforting to ride without the windows blacked out and I marvelled at the green fields all around me, some filled with livestock, others bursting with crops, while my three children slept, Emily and James on the seats in front of me, Rhona in my lap. When we finally reached what looked to be the centre of Bryn, I noticed a large CO-OP store, a few pubs and a few shops, but not a good deal else.

I heard the Wigan dialect for the first time when the friendly driver welcomed us aboard. He took Emily's little hand in his, smiling so as not to alarm her and softening his voice when he looked up and spoke to me,

"Artawreet Mrs?"

I had absolutely no idea what he'd said, it sounded like double Dutch to me, but I smiled and asked him if we'd far to go and he answered by saying.

"Nay Mrs!" That I managed to understand, "you and the kiddies must be klempt, you poor buggers."

"We are that," I answered, assuming klempt meant tired, but I was to discover many new words and eventually get my head around the accent. 'Klempt' was a word they used for very hungry and when he used the word 'artawreet' he was merely asking me if I was alright.

I only hoped that Mrs Lea was a patient lady with not quite as broad an accent as our driver.

I was to find Bryn a close knit community of hardworking people. Many of them worked the land and provided precious foodstuffs for the war effort and, like the people from Harrogate Street, they were genuine to the core.

The driver, carried Emily in his outstretched arms and I managed to rouse my son who held onto my coat tails as we made our way to the detached house, in the pitch darkness, him stumbling as I struggled with Rhona. Suddenly a shaft of light lit up our pathway as the front door opened and a slight, round faced lady with snow white hair, tied up in a bun, stood framed in the light. I squinted up at her, but couldn't make out her features.

"Welcome to my home Anne," she uttered with only a trace of the Wigan accent, one I had no difficulty understanding. She then moved to greet me and took Rhona from my arms, kissing my right cheek and as she did, I reached for my son's hand and pulled him inside, quickly followed by the driver, still carrying Emily, who slept soundly in his arms.

We were shown to a large bedroom that must have been four times the size of my own back in Liverpool. It was so large that it contained a double bed, plus two singles.

"I know it doesn't look much." Mrs Lea told me, "but the beds are very comfortable. Why don't you get the children settled and join me in the kitchen? We can have a drink and a chat as soon as you're ready love."

I did as she suggested and only hoped our chat wouldn't take too long as I was bone tired.

Very soon afterwards I found my way to the large kitchen and was presented with a huge mug of *Ovaltine.*

"I hope you don't mind Anne but I've taken the liberty of adding a little something to the mix. I'm sure it'll help you sleep and you look like you need it. It's hard work bringing up children when there's two parents, goodness knows how you're managing," she said, her comments leading me to believe the authorities had told her plenty about our personal circumstances.

To be honest, I was beyond caring as the warm liquid began to loosen up my joints and work its way to my toes. All at once I was ready to curl up and sleep and remember little else of what my gracious host said.

8

The sunlight streamed into our bedroom and as I awakened I momentarily lost my bearings. Opening my eyes a feeling of disorientation overwhelmed me. Where was I? Nothing in the room looked or felt familiar. I pulled myself into a sitting position and in seconds I'd remembered.

"Mummy, I'm in my own bed," Emily suddenly piped up, "and I love it."

"That's lovely Em. 'Ow about climbin' in 'ere and givin' your old mum a cuddle? We won't tell the other two," I whispered.

She couldn't wait to snuggle up beside me, fully aware her sister had taken up most of my time since her birth. I took her tiny frame in my arms and marvelled at the sweet smell of her body and hair. How could a child sleep for hours and still smell so good?

"You know you'll always be my special girl don't you Em?" I told her, my eyes welling up as I stroked her thick mop of dark brown hair and looked down at the features that reminded me so much of Angus, even though people told me my eldest daughter was the spit of me.

She was silent for a moment, but held onto me, her tiny hands a huge comfort to me.

"Will I ever see my Daddy again?"

"Of course you will. What makes you ask such a thing?"

"I just get scared that he'll be made dead in the war."

I looked down at her, but she hid her face, probably remembering her Mother possessed a quick and violent temper.

"That won't 'appen. Your Dad'll be home sooner than you know Em."

She looked up at me, her big brown eyes meeting mine.

"Do you promise mummy?"

I swallowed a number of times before meeting her gaze and finally answered.

"I can't promise Em," I said, "but I 'ave a very strong feelin' that he'll be comin' back to us and when I get one of my special feelin's I'm never wrong."

"I'm glad Mummy," she said, somehow comforted by my honesty.

It took us some time, but I got the children washed and dressed and then made myself presentable, smelling breakfast cooking below stairs. Mrs Lea was bright eyed and bushy tailed and greeted us all with a smile.

"Sleep well?"

"Smashin' thanks," I answered, then with my eyes straying to the cups and plates and the stove. "What can I do?"

"No dear, you sit and see to the little ones. You must be tired after such a long journey. Will the baby take some toast and a soft boiled egg?"

"That'll be just lovely," I replied wanting to thank her, but also wanting to let her know that I'd do my bit and I didn't think it was the time to mention how faddy Rhona could be. "I want to 'elp, cook, clean, whatever needs doin'," I went on, "I want to repay your kindness."

"We'll talk about all of that later love, let's get some breakfast inside of us and we'll have a little chat while the children are playing," she said and, as she served up the crusty doorsteps of homemade bread and boiled eggs, I exhaled and tried to relax.

9

We had our chat and agreed to share the household duties including cooking. Mrs Lea, who was not a good sleeper and therefore an early riser, insisted on making breakfast for all of us each morning. We agreed to work together on lunch, but I was to be responsible for the evening meal. The advantage I had was that fresh vegetables and meat were much easier to come by in rural Wigan and I no longer needed to scratch around for things to cobble together. I hadn't cooked like that for years. In Bryn it wasn't quite what you'd call a black market, more a grey one. People had their ration books just as we did back in Liverpool, but either grew vegetables or kept livestock, or if not, knew how to come by both, through contacts within the community.

Mrs Lea was a good cook and we shared tips as we grew as thick as thieves. She showed me how to mix herbs for a variety of ailments and insisted that we all drank a special mixture of her own each day before breakfast. I never knew what was in it, but it must have been good stuff as none of us were ever sick when we stayed with her.

There was no longer any need to make blind stew and every meal seemed to feature fresh meat, be it mutton, rabbit, duck, chicken or beef. The children were also flourishing in the fresh air and it was comforting to sit and rest up, or catch up with a bit of darning without worrying about the constant threat of air raids. It was always possible, of course, that a stray bomb or two might find its way to us and Mrs Lea was prepared. She'd had an Anderson shelter constructed at the bottom of her enormous garden. Back home it was a good idea to always have the children in your sights, just in case the Germans decided to deliver more gifts.

I grew fond of the easier way of life and I think our host was happy to have the company and didn't seem troubled by my two noisy toddlers and their baby sister. An example of her kindness was when she provided clogs for Emily and James one day. But this was typical of the woman, noticing that their shoes were falling apart and ill fitting, she'd clearly spoken to the local clog maker and called in a favour. When presented with the clogs, both James and Emily giggled at the sight of this strange new footwear and Emily piped up,

"They're likes elves shoes mummy," and proceeded to clomp about in them, enchanted by the noise they made indoors.

I watched them both learning how to walk in their new footwear, remembering my own childhood and the wooden clogs I wore, which were much more commonplace amongst the working classes then. They must have taken a bit of getting used for a child who normally wore proper leather shoes, but there was little alternative unless you had pots of money, as raw materials were near impossible to get hold of during wartime.

Mrs Lea was a widow and her only child, a son; was overseas fighting the enemy. She didn't like to talk about her husband's passing or her son very often and I respected her wishes. I assumed this was because each subject was painful for her and I also worked out she was very much a person who lived in the present.

As the weeks passed, she'd tell me snippets about her early life and include bits and pieces about Bryn's foibles and its history. She explained the place had once been known as Bryn Cross and still was by some locals. She also told me that around 1250 AD, Peter-De-Brynne, a local man of wealth and position; arranged the marriage of his daughter to a man from the wealthy Gerard family and the locals claim the name of Bryn was founded upon their union. She'd also tell me little things like the regular smashing of the window of the shop that stood on the corner of Warrington Road and Gerard Street in the town centre. This she declared was caused by the trolly buses (a bit like trams) coming off their rails and careering into the shop as they took the sharp corner too fast.

Our daily routine was to rise early, take breakfast, then send the children off to play. We'd then go through the big house sweeping and dusting and washing the pots, plus we'd make up the ingredients for the next day's bread. We'd then start the day's baking, which could include small pies, cakes or scones. That would usually take us to lunchtime, although to be fair we'd normally have a cuppa and a homemade scone around eleven. We'd then work together on lunch, consisting of a sandwich made from the previous day's bread and huge chunks of locally produced cheese, washed down with fresh milk. We'd normally eat them with homemade piccalilli, (Which was basically cabbage, tomatoes, celery and onions, plus mustard, flour, vinegar, salt and pepper) or pickle (which was slightly different, using carrots, swede or turnip, apples, cauliflower, onion, plus sugar, salt and vinegar) and I can tell you I'd never tasted anything so delicious. We'd take the children shopping usually in the afternoon and come back in time for me to start the evening meal. Mrs Lea would then wash any clothing or sheets, something she preferred to do herself, even though she included any clothing and sheets of ours. I can picture her now with a bowl of steaming water and her mangle, with a scarf tied to her head, smiling back at me as I prepared the last meal of the day.

When the children were asleep, we'd retire to the parlour like two old maids and listen to the wireless together. We'd usually have a tipple from a variety of dusty old bottles marked with hand written labels in a spidery hand. One would say rhubarb, another elderflower, another gooseberry and so on. It was homemade wine, all made from local ingredients and although the first mouthful often tasted a bit funny, it was certainly potent stuff and I never remember having any trouble sleeping after a glass of it.

One such evening sticks in my mind vividly and for reasons I will explain, I count that incident as one of the pivotal moments of my life, it changed everything and charted the course that my life would take.

10

The children were all soundly asleep. Even little Rhona who seemed to suffer with her chest in the City was a regular sleeper in this fabulous country air and her breathing was always easier.

We listened to the likes of *Back Room Boy* on the wireless starring *Arthur Askey* and *Crooks Tour* with *Basil Radford* and *Naughton Lane*, then as usual Mrs Lea insisted we'd tune into Pope Pius XII's broadcast from the Vatican, fully aware of the mystery surrounding my husband's wherebaouts. I was concentrating so hard as I always did, that when I heard mention of a familiar name, I was stunned. His serial number meant nothing to me. My head was spinning, but I didn't know whether it was from the wine or good old fashioned panic.

"Anne? Wasn't that him?"

I couldn't speak, my mind was reeling in several different directions, my hands suddenly clammy. Eventually I was able to focus.

"My God e's alive," I eventually said.

The pope was reading through a list of Prisoners of War in Italy and to my great delight he confirmed Angus was alive. There was no other information. Had he been injured? Where had he been captured?

Mrs Lea stood and reached for the raisin wine and brought it to me.

"This calls for a celebration I think Anne. Sorry I don't have any champagne."

As she refilled my glass, tears of joy sprang from my eyes and although I was so pleased to learn he was alive, relief was my biggest emotion. I hadn't admitted to myself he could have been dead these past months, but subconsciously I dreaded the worst news of all.

"Oh come here love and give us a hug," my host said to me and I did as requested.

Two further glasses of wine later and I was safely tucked up in my bed.

I didn't remember much about the previous evening, I only recall waking with a splitting headache and seeing Emily and James standing in front of me fully dressed.

"We've had our breakfast mummy," Emily told me.

"Oh mummy must have overslept." I responded in a croaky voice.

"No Mrs Lea told us to let you sleep, she said you had a bit of a cold," James added, a worried look on his face.

"Yes erm, that's right I do, but I feel a lot better for the extra sleep," I lied.

"Mum, I had a dream last night about Dad. In it he told me to tell you he was alright," my son explained, a rather puzzled look on his face.

"It doesn't surprise me," I said ruffling his hair, "And d'you both want to know a secret?"

"Yes!" they both called out.

"I 'ave it on good authority thar 'e is alright and we're going to write to 'im and tell 'im all about your dream once I get 'is new address."

When I did finally roused myself I was presented with another glass of raisin wine and just the smell of it made me gag. I pushed it away.

"No love you must drink it. Even if it takes you half an hour, get it down you and keep it down and you'll be as right as rain for the rest of the day," Mrs Lea assured me.

It was a real effort to drink and an even taller order to keep down, but by lunchtime I was feeling more like my old self and ready for some food.

In the afternoon there was plenty to organise. Instead of pulling my weight Mrs Lea sent me off to town. I arranged for a telegram to be sent to James and Emily, briefly explaining what I'd learned about Angus and asking them to let Groves know. I then spent some time drafting a letter informing the war office and asked them if they could let me know of his whereabouts and condition as soon as possible. When I got back, Mrs Lea had not only washed all of our dirty clothes, but had even cooked our evening meal - a great enormous meat pie and boiled potatoes with carrots. What a feast it was.

"I owe you so much today. Thank you for everythin'," I blabbered, close to tears and mental exhaustion.

"Give over Anne. I know you'd do the same for me if roles were reversed. Now eat up and I'll tell you about my plans for tomorrow.

She explained she'd invited a few close friends over to celebrate my good news and went onto to say we'd have a good old fashioned knees-up. I could say nothing other than 'thanks again' to this remarkable woman.

*

    Mrs Lea, true to her word, introduced me to her friends the very next afternoon. They were, Mrs Woodcock, a friendly face I recognised from the post office, Mr and Mrs Gregory, a jolly couple in their fifties who had a local farm and old Tom, the bus driver, whose broad accent was no easier to understand. Despite his age, (which I was reliably informed was sixty-four) Tom made the local milk deliveries and helped out on the Gregory farm, on top of driving the local bus. I was also to learn that this sprightly man was responsible for the homemade wine we drank each evening.
    That morning we made the house ship shape and Bristol fashion, but as the sky looked clear, it was hoped we'd spend the afternoon in the garden. We baked savoury and sweet pies, put out bread and cheese and made up a salad adding some hard boiled eggs.
    I was enjoying myself, the weight of my main worry having been lifted and the children played together on the soft, dry grass. Mrs Woodcock, after more than one or two glasses from a new batch of blackcurrant wine, sidled up to me and proceeded to tell me out of the corner of her mouth, that she had it on good authority that old Tom had his eye on Mrs Lea. Although they were both widowed, she went on, she gave him no encouragement whatsoever,
    "But he's a stubborn old bugger and doesn't give up easily," she went on, nudging my elbow in the direction of the two of them. We watched as Mrs Lea was cutting him a slice of rhubarb pie, oblivious to his bright blue eyes following her every movement. I had to concede, there seemed to be something in what I'd been told, but I felt uncomfortable gossiping about a woman who had shown me nothing but kindness.
    As though he was aware of what we were discussing, Tom turned on his heel and marched over to us, holding his plate of pie and fork close to his face.
    "Take no notice of this old bint," he announced with a twinkle in his eye, "She's just moochin'."

Mrs Gregory explained to me later that 'moochin'' meant being nosey, so maybe Tom did know what Mrs Woodcock was telling me, but more than likely he knew her well enough to guess.

Her face altered and she flushed slightly.

"Will yer' look at her Anne? She can't take the truth and now she's got a monk on," Tom added, laughing into his plate. He then proceeded to shovel the contents of it into his mouth, keeping a close eye on Mrs Woodcock, who continued with her 'monk on', which meant, of course, that she was sulking.

The afternoon extended into early evening and Mr and Mrs Gregory made their excuses, claiming they needed to rise early, which I didn't doubt was true. Tom took the slightly swaying Mrs Woodcock by the arm and said,

"I think this silly old bint has supped a bit too much. I better get her home I expect," he added, failing to mention he'd supped just as much if not more, yet the alcohol seemed to be having little or no effect on him.

"Alsithy," was his final word and he took Mrs Woodcock by the arm and ushered her towards a battered old van.

Mrs Lea frowned as she watched her friend supported by old Tom.

It was impossible to read her thoughts, but she caught me looking and offered me a tired smile.

"She's a terrible gossip and can't hold her drink, but she's got a big heart Anne," she sighed. "Did you enjoy it love?"

I moved closer and put my arm around her shoulder.

"It was wonderful. Thank you so much."

We walked back to the house and stared the process of clearing up. She then insisted on washing the pots as I washed the children and prepared them for bed. They were asleep in no time.

I joined Mrs Lea in the parlour and we decided on tea, both admitting we'd had our fill of homemade wine for the day.

It was another peaceful end to the day and for the first time in months my mind was able to function properly. I even allowed myself to imagine the war ending and Angus coming home to us, but little did I know that almost three more years of war in Europe would keep us apart.

Anne catching up on the news

Angus's Story - part 3

1

I was taken prisoner by the Germans at a place called Knightsbridge, near Tobruk. It was 6th June 1942 and by 5.00pm after a fierce battle in which we suffered heavy casualties, the skirmish was over. We were a rag tag band of soldiers and many like myself had been wounded, but this meant nothing to the men holding guns over us.

A rumour circulated, as these things do, that the Germans were going to shoot us all. The theory was Rommel's men had no rations or transport for Prisoners of War and as such there was only one solution. That particular myth was dispelled when those of us who could walk were marched into the desert at gunpoint, under the full glare of the North African sun. We marched for five miles, a slowly weaving snake of camouflaged men, moving deep behind enemy lines, as our German counterparts kept their rifles trained on us from the relative comfort of their armoured vehicles.

We were given nothing to eat or drink, but no man complained. We were too exhausted to waste energy on speech and every man fell asleep on the sand when the seemingly never-ending march was brought to a stop.

I had no idea how bad my head wound was, but the bleeding had stopped. I knew that much. It was a case of surviving at all costs. Yet when they woke us at 7.00am to commence marching again, we were badly in need of food and water. Many of us hadn't eaten for twenty-four hours, yet the lack of water was by far our biggest problem in the unforgiving heat. We marched another 7 miles, many of us moving at a snail's pace, on instinct alone. We stopped again as darkness fell and mercifully we were each given a biscuit and about one third of a pint of water each. We knew this gesture might keep some of us alive and we ate and drank in absolute silence, grateful for the sustenance.

As night fell my mind drifted to the dead boy, who'd taken the shell fragment meant for me, but I forced myself to be strong and pushed any thoughts like this out of my mind. My badly dehydrated body could ill afford to shed a tear, although God knows I could have cried a river of them for the loss of the boy's life. I wondered what had become of Jimmy and big Ted, had they survived? I could only hope and pray they were both still breathing, but I feared for Jim Kite, remembering he'd also been hit.

Despite my fatigue I found it difficult to find sleep and I lay on my back and looked into the stars that lit up the night sky above me, marvelling at its vastness. Compared to the millions of stars in the sky, earth seemed to be nothing more than a grain of sand in the desert and, not for the first time, the futility of war weighed upon my mind. Instead of half starving out here in the middle of nowhere, a man my age should be with his children looking up at the solar system and sleeping in his own bed with his wife, rather than lying on a bed of sand, next to a stinking soldier.

I found sleep holding that thought and perhaps for that reason dreamed the war was over. I was in uniform and my heart was swelling with emotion as my heavy boots clumped on the cobbles of Harrogate Street, knowing I was moments away from a reunion with my wife and kids. As I approached my home and knocked on the door, the sky overhead suddenly darkened and there was no answer, puzzled, I knocked again - still nothing. In frustration, I pushed at the door and thought I could hear screams coming from inside. Panic welled up inside me and I began to beat at the door, attempting to force it open with my shoulder. This time I could hear the licking and crackling of fire on the inside, yet the more I struggled the more rigid the door became.

All at once I was shaken awake by a soldier who had been sleeping nearby.

"Quiet down lad. Ssshhh. You'll have us all shot for disturbing their beauty sleep."

I had apparently been screaming Anne's name aloud.

I apologised and fell back into a dreamless sleep almost immediately.

2

Next morning we were met by a convoy of armoured trucks and herded aboard them like cattle and driven to a place called Bomba, near Timimi, situated in what we call Libya today. There we were ordered out of the trucks and forced to sit on the ground, under the watchful eye of a handful of armed guards. We were given yet another biscuit each, but half a pint of water each this time. Once we'd eaten and enjoyed every last drop of our water ration, a German medic moved amongst us and began examining each man for any sign of wounding or injury. He was a slight man, with thinning blonde hair that was the colour of the sand. He spoke a little English and he treated the men with respect and empathy.

When he came to me, he took some time exploring my head wound and after some time, he looked into my brown eyes and said,

"You have, how do you say? Pieces from the bomb in your head."

"Shrapnel in my head?"

"Yes it is correct. You will need to be taken to hospital to have it fixed. It will be alright I think."

"Thank you Doctor," I replied, as he moved to the next man.

Along with the other wounded men I was put back on the same truck that had brought me this far and I looked on as the men who had come with me were left behind. I was not to meet up with any of them again.

The trucks brought us to a German hospital at Derna, a coastal town in the Libyan region of Cyrenaica, that was a German stronghold in the early part of the conflict. Here they also had a munitions depot and an airstrip.

We were housed on a ward totally comprising of prisoners, yet the place was clean and bright and there were real beds to sleep in. We were cleaned up and given gowns to wear with no under clothing. Our soiled uniforms were removed and we didn't see them again until we were well enough to leave and that first night it was an absolute pleasure to sleep in a real bed, with clean sheets. I slept as soundly as a baby.

The following day I was brought to an examination room by a friendly faced nurse, where a fat German Doctor picked at my wound and then set about removing metal fragments from my skull. He said nothing to me and gave me nothing for the pain, as he set about his task with great determination, only ever speaking to bark curt instructions at the nurse. He finally cleaned the wound up and left the room briskly, without so much as a glance in my direction.

The nurse who had been the subject of his petulance smiled sweetly at me and wheeled me back to the ward. After helping me into my bed, she peered into my bloodshot eyes and handed me two capsules and a glass of water.

"For de pain. You take now, yes?"

I nodded and forced the horse pills down my dry throat. In minutes I became drowsy and drifted into a drug-induced slumber.

I stayed there for four days until the same autocratic Doctor examined me again and then roared out his instructions to the nurse. Before I knew it, my uniform was returned and a German guard appeared at my bedside and instructed me to dress and go with him.

I was taken to a compound filled to the brim with morose prisoners, none of whom I'd met before. The place was a series of empty wooden huts. I found a space on the floor and lay down on the coarse wood, suddenly feeling tired and in some pain again; recent experiences seemingly had taken their toll upon me. I put my hands into the pockets of my uniform that had been cleaned, although it was still stained with blood, some of which was my own. I found six of the horse pills the kind nurse had clearly slipped into my pocket. I lay there, smiling, for the first time in weeks, pleased to discover that human kindness was still a commodity to be found, even in the crudest of situations.

3

I stayed at the camp for only two days and I was glad of this. The place was no more than a stopgap for prisoners of war, who were being shipped to a variety of locations. I made no friends and in truth hardly spoke to anyone, for although the pain in my head was beginning to recede, I was in no shape to be my usual gregarious self.

On my third day there I was instructed to pack my meagre things together and given one days' ration, consisting of a 6oz loaf of stale white bread and a tin of bully beef. Quite how they decided who went where I would never know, but I was glad to be leaving that dull place behind and happily climbed aboard the usual cattle truck.

It arrived in Benghazi, one of the oldest Libyan cities, standing on the banks of the Mediterranean at around 10 o'clock that night and we were herded into another faceless compound, surrounded by barbed wire which housed the same wooden huts. I wasn't given any time to familiarise myself with my surroundings, for after a reasonable night's sleep on the floor, we were roused again and once more herded onto the same trucks.

We travelled for a full day again to a place called Sutern, which was about 80 miles from Tripoli, again arriving after nightfall. Our disjointed band of soldiers, were suffering from fatigue, thirst and hunger, but sleep was all we were offered. We spent six days in this new camp and nobody stated whether this was our final destination or not, but I would have been surprised, as not one man from my regiment was present.

The chaps at this camp seemed a brighter bunch and they shared scant news of the conflict, cigarettes and what little sustenance and water they could. Card schools were everywhere, playing for no more than matchsticks and makeshift games of football were arranged, playing with coconuts provided by the guards. It was the oddest game with such a misshapen ball, but men in such circumstances did anything to pass the time.

There was never any talk of escape here. For one thing there was nowhere to run but the desert and without food and water only a fool would attempt it. For that reason the security at such camps was quite relaxed. We were the lucky ones. Many of our comrades had died and every man had lost a close friend or two and deep down in a place nobody would ever talk about, a man was thankful he was still breathing. It was too early for men with those thoughts to risk certain death, but as time moves on and incarceration begins to eat away at you, there is a natural desire to be free and this unquenchable craving forces a man to take risks.

    It was no different for me.

4

After three weeks at that hell hole, five hundred of us were reprieved and taken in trucks to yet another camp where conditions were only slightly better. The camp was called Trig Taruna, a small, nondescript place that was only a few kilometres from Tripoli.

The food was no better and there remained a lack of medical care, but there was no overcrowding and the majority of the prisoners already at this camp were as healthy as we were, even though every man was quite obviously losing weight. I was settled into barracks with men from my own regiment and I would call the men I bunked with acquaintances rather than friends. Nevertheless, it was pleasing to have men alongside me, who could appreciate what we'd been though. This camaraderie was impossible to beat and to say we took comfort in each other's presence is a massive understatement. We'd faced the enemy together and lived to tell the tale and such a shared experience tended to bond a group of men.

About a week later, more men were brought to Trig Taruna and as there was never very much to do, I sauntered over to the fence and watched the men disembark from the dusty trucks. I was smoking a cigarette I'd bummed from a young Irish lad who never seemed short of anything, he was what I'd call a wheeler dealer back at home, but here a system of barter existed for most of what he could get his hands on in camp. For example, he'd trade soap for razor blades, or cigarettes for comic books and so on. If you needed or wanted something bad enough, he could get it for you at a price.

I was enjoying the smoke, but even though I was only half way through it I let it fall to the ground before me as my mouth fell open. Striding only yards from me, as large as life, was big Ted, his gargantuan frame unmistakable. He didn't see me, but a broad grin filled my face at the sight of a man who had become my true friend these past two years.

"You alright there Angus? That ciggy wasn't one a' those funny ones was it now? If it was, I might want to trade it back, seeing as half of it's still burning in the dust," said the Irish wheeler.

Fixed on my own agenda, without realising it I ignored him and raced back to where my Commanding Officer was situated.

The man was only a sergeant but he was the most senior ranking man from our regiment and as such the chain of command fell to him. He was a good man and listened to my request, then stood and said he'd speak with the others, but didn't forsee any problems.

Half an hour later, Ted walked through the gate, dwarfing the other men with him. He looked thinner than I remembered and his face was pinched.

I ran towards him and, as soon as he saw me, tears welled up in his eyes and he lifted me off the ground, like the big bear of a man he was.

"I thought you was a goner Angus. I saw you and the lad hit and thought that was it. Oh God man, it's good to see you in one piece."

"Same here Ted, but put me down now will you? I can hardly breathe."

"Oh sorry, you know me, I don't know my own strength," he apologised, then placed me back onto the ground. "Are any of the others 'ere?"

"Some, but not many," I told him, then asked him the one burning question I had stored up. "Any word of Jimmy Kite?"

"None, but I know he was hit too. When all hell broke loose, I lost sight of both of you."

I managed a weak smile.

"Come on Ted, let's get out of the sun and get your gear stowed and I'll re-introduce you to what's left of the chaps."

He followed me into the barracks, and the sergeant had been as good as his word and arranged for him to bunk on the floor next to me, the men had moved up to accommodate him.

"What's the food like 'ere?" he asked.

"Bloody awful."

I looked across at him and that same pinched expression filled his thinning face.

Just as I thought, he was starving.

5

I'd managed to get my hands on some paper and a couple of biros and for some reason I began to put together an account of my experiences since my capture. Morbidly, I thought it might be something the children could have, if for some reason I didn't make it back home. But that was not my only motive. I wanted a record of what I'd been through, but not necessarily to share with anyone in particular. I hoped by writing a detailed description of it all I could file it all away and get on with my life. But I was forced to deal with the usual joshing from the other blokes and although they were only being playful, I thought some remarks were uncalled for. Things like; 'Oh look Gus is writing a letter to the Commandant asking to be excused from parade for a week,'

'Don't look now lads, but Angus is writing another love letter to Ted. But the floor'll never withstand both their weight'

I continued on regardless and tried to let it wash over me.

We'd spent a month at Trig Taruna when we were instructed to prepare for a short journey to Tripoli. We were taken to the docks and put aboard a ship bound for Italy. I for one was glad to be leaving the stink of Libya behind, a place I would be happy never to see again. The conditions onboard ship were crude, but the sea was mercifully calm and even the men without sea legs managed to survive the voyage without too much trouble.

We docked at Naples on August 2nd 1942 and the landscape that greeted us was a welcome change from the dust bowl of North Africa. It was still unspeakably warm, but the blue waters and the sight of trees, fragrant flowers and green fields in the distance was a sight to behold. The view was simply breathtaking and even though this was enemy territory, it felt that we were much closer to our own way of life. I had never been happier to call myself a European.

We were given a hot shower shortly after we disembarked and weretaken by train to a place called Capua. I felt cleaner than I had in months and it seemed the Italians, at least, wanted to treat us like civilised human beings. Capua was about sixteen miles from Naples and although we didn't see much of it, it was a place steeped in history and was once the second city of the Italian peninsula.

Here we were sorted into regiments and billeted in tents. It was pleasant enough, though, in the tents, cool and fragrant at night, as oppose to freezing in the desert and the tents afforded us a little more privacy. A few days later, Red Cross parcels were distributed at a ratio of one to every five men, plus each man was given ten cigarettes. This, coupled with our Italian food ration, meant that we didn't go hungry, least of all Ted of course, who unashamedly gobbled down any scraps of food left by men from our regiment.

    Once more, the regime was a relaxed affair and the view was a thousand times better, but boredom soon set in and the usual card schools, petty squabbles and gambling for cigarettes was the core activity of our group. I kept myself to myself more or less, happier with one of my closest friends at hand and free from pain. I joined in some of the activities such as football, but also concentrated on bringing my journal up to date. I also had a little more time for solitary contemplation and wondered long and often about Anne and the children. I tried to imagine how tall five year old James was now and how he looked, and wondered if Emily, who was now three, had altered beyond all recognition these past two years, but I could put no face to Rhona. The war had stolen the early years of her life from me and I could not forsee how much longer it would keep me from seeing my youngest child. On my blackest days I fretted that Rhona's estrangement from her Father might affect her development.

6

On 2nd of October, a little more than five hundred of us moved from Capua and I for one was sorry to be leaving the place. We were taken by train to a newly built concentration camp in a place called Macerata and we were the first prisoners to set foot in the place. Macerata is the provincial capital of a place called Le Marche and is a hilly location overlooking the beautiful, blue waters of the Adriatic Sea.

There was the usual search before we were taken to our billets. As we entered the compound, the familiar sight of row upon row of wooden huts was a foreboding prospect, but once we were taken inside we were pleasantly surprised to find real beds to sleep in. Apart from those of us who'd spent any time in hospital, it had been an awfully long time since we'd slept in real beds and no matter how uncomfortable they might be, a real bed always beat the hard ground.

Two days later, every man received his own Red Cross food parcel and fifty cigarettes.

Things had certainly started well and a feeling of optimism circulated throughout the camp. More prisoners began to arrive and, as always, a way of relieving the monotony was to watch the new arrivals come in and we'd often play a game of guessing the nationality of each group. Granted, it was often easy to recognise the uniform, but the men who arrived in small groups were more difficult to pinpoint.

The number grew to around 8,000 men and it was obvious to every man the camp was overcrowded, but as I started to receive mail from home, I was initially oblivious to the problems overcapacity created.

In her first letter, Anne explained how she'd learned that I was a prisoner of war by listening to the Vatican radio. Then she told me that she and the children had been evacuated to Wigan and everyone was happy and healthy. The letter was filled with facts about the conflict and I suspected Anne's earlier stabs at propaganda were continuing. Although, I had to agree with her when she suggested we were now gaining the upper hand, after being on the back foot for so many years. She'd told me General Montgomery had taken control of the eighth army in North Africa in early August and the conflict was beginning to swing our way. This was strengthened by the fact that Monty had driven Rommel back following the battle for Alam Halfa, in early September.

I was to learn much later from Peter, who was engaged in the fight in North Africa, that our firepower was now superior and our numbers had swelled, allowing Monty to turn the tables on the Germans and out manoeuvre them. Now it was our chance to turn the screw.

I was happier than I'd been in a long time as Christmas grew nearer. My family were out of harm's way and we appeared to be winning the war. Anne had also sent me a photograph of herself and the children. It became my most treasured possession. Anne was seated, holding Rhona in her arms, and James and Emily were flanking her. Just looking at it would make the hairs on the back of my neck stand up and I can tell you I shed a tear or two of joy as I lay in my bunk, staring at the images until my eyes could take no more and I'd drop seamlessly into sleep.

My joy knew no bounds when my Mother sent me a long and well-written letter that seemed to echo the optimism about our efforts in the war. She told me news about the family. Father was well and keeping busy. Mr. Groves also was getting along without Anne and Tommy, and it seemed he and Father had become quite thick these past years. Jack was doing his bit in the RAF, somewhere in Scotland, and Peter was with Monty in North Africa. Margie and Albert were *Derby and Joan* according to Mother and planned to marry next year. She was working in civil defence and Albert was waiting for confirmation of his call up to India with the Air force, where he was to operate as a cook. This pleased me, as I was very fond of my only sister and remembered Albert seemed a smashing bloke.

I enjoyed Christmas of 1942 much more than I expected to. My entire family were thriving and this I knew was rare during war time.

Yet, little did I realise, that an ill wind was brewing, bringing with it some of the blackest times I would know.

7

The weather was temperate when we arrived at Macerata in October, but by December it was advisable to wrap up when out of doors. In the distance, the mountains were delightfully snow-capped. The weather, though, deteriorated in December and February and, as if to test our resolve even more, the expected arrival of Red Cross food parcels failed to materialise. Rumours circulated that the guards had intercepted our parcels to feed their families, although this was never proven.

Rations were of poor quality and it became survival of the fittest as we struggled for sustenance and proper clothing with which to keep ourselves warm.

Over sixty men died due to malnutrition and some of the dead were from my regiment. They were men with wives and loved ones waiting at home, men with hope for a better future, no different from myself and Ted, but they were gone and it was totally unnecessary. I was deeply depressed and prayed for warmer weather.

I received my first next of kin parcel in late February and it included new underclothing that was both warm and badly needed. In March I received another, plus five cigarette parcels, including one courtesy of the regiment.

As the weather slowly improved through March and April, some men who were suffering started to recover and spirits in the camp began to lift. Time passed very slowly and Ted and I elected to volunteer for farm work to try and break the monotony and also in the hope we might expand our meagre food rations. To be truthful, Ted was not keen on it, but I'd heard that food was plentiful on the farm and I had an idea that Ted would benefit from the work. He'd become morose and listless and not simply because of the lack of food. The conditions at camp had also hit him badly and I thought a change of scenery would do us both good.

Anne's letters continued, giving me sporadic updates concerning the children during the early part of 1943, plus her own particular brand of propaganda. It seemed to be good news all around, starting with the Russians fighting back in Stalingrad around 10th January. Then in late January, Montgomery's eighth army took Tripoli and I found myself elated, but frustrated by the stretch of water that separated me from my British brothers at arms. In early February the Germans surrendered at Stalingrad, which was the first major setback in Russia for Mr. Hitler. The Soviet troops then continued to press their advantage by taking Kursk a week later.

In early March, the Germans withdrew from Tunisia and it was clear to me the tide really was turning in our favour. The combined powers of Britain, America and Russia seemed to be turning the war our way at last.

My last memory of the camp was taking part in a specially arranged game of football against the guards. The best eleven we could muster were selected and I was proud to play at inside right, reminding my compatriots I was one of the oldest men to take the field.

The Italians sported none other than the Italian national goalkeeper, *Guiseppe Meazza*; who was a camp guard. The man had hands like shovels and I worried we might not be able to score. The match as you might imagine, was fiercely contested. The Italians sat deep and our game in retort was high tempo. We peppered their goal with shots, but we were susceptible to the counter attack and at half time with a lot of energy expended, we were one - nil down.

During the half time team talk our C.O., no doubt remembering he was in fact a sergeant-major, ripped into us with a ferocity none of us had ever before encountered. He reminded us this was more than a football match, we were at battle with the enemy and went on to finish his rousing speech by playing on the fact that we were up against free men; men who knew nothing of our hardships.

His words stung and catapulted us into action.

We laid into them in the same vein as the second half opened, but with a will of iron burning in each man's eye. After ten minutes the ball fell loose from a corner and dropped to me twenty five yards out. I'd like to say I remembered to keep my head down, or that I picked my spot like the great footballers of my day. The truth is I hit the ball so sweetly, that the moment I connected with it, I knew it was a goal and the fact that it travelled so well was a pure fluke as far as I was concerned. I kept this knowledge to myself though, as my teammates went wild. Italian national goalkeeper or not, we held them until the final whistle and we embraced our fellow players, each team totally drained.

But despite what had been said at the interval, for ninety minutes we were just twenty two men playing a game and each man was the better for it.

8

On the 12th May 1943, forty of us were moved on to a working camp at San Bernadino, one of the most northerly points of Italy. The location was close to the border with Switzerland and a rural location, about 75 miles from Turin.

We were billeted at a village called Marengo and I was appointed as cook for the men. Rations were much more generous, plus our Red Cross parcels were a lot more regular. We had potatoes and vegetables that had been taken from the earth that day and there always seemed to be poultry or game available, to add to our overflowing plates. This was no surprise as the woodland surrounding the village was filled with wild life and the villagers were generous people. My lack of skill in the culinary department seemed not to matter, as the men in our small company were looking fitter and a healthier than they had for months and Ted no longer had that pinched look on his face.

I was still receiving plenty of mail and an occasional book parcel. You can't imagine what this meant to a man like me, who during peacetime read whatever he could lay his hands on and adored literature in all its forms. Even the opening of the parcel excited me, but it was more than that, it was a realisation that the things we'd previously taken for granted were now so precious.

Anne and Mother's reports told of the eighth army's advance in North Africa. By 7th May we'd taken Tunisia with the assistance of the Yanks. But the best news of all filtered through when the Germans and Italians jointly surrendered in North Africa on 13th May 1943. We had to keep the noise down, but the villagers saw to it we had wine with our rations that night. The locals seemed as happy as we were the conflict was swinging our way. Perhaps like all working people, they just wanted it to end and for life to return to normal.

We continued to work in the fields, growing closer to the friendly villagers, who it seemed couldn't do enough to assist us. Our health and spirits couldn't have been stronger when word reached us the Allies had captured Sicily on 22nd July and then three days later, Mussolini and his fascist government had been overthrown by Marshal Pietro Badoglio, who it was rumoured was negotiating with the Allies.

We didn't know it then, but we were to face further trials and our return to health and fitness could not have come at a better time.

9

News continued to filter in that the Allies had advanced into Italy and by Septempter 9th 1943, Salerno and Taranto had been taken, which meant they were taking Italy from the direction we had arrived. For us, the great day arrived at Marengo the next day, when news reached us Italy had ceased fighting and we were considered free men. The sparse contingent of Italian guards who looked after us simply evaporated overnight. We packed our belongings and freed ourselves from San Bernadino camp. Ted, myself and two other chaps made our way to the village, intending to hide there for a few days, word having reached us that German troops were patrolling and were on the lookout for escaped prisoners.

The villagers remained extremely helpful and shielded us to begin with, taking all of us into their homes, even providing us with civilian clothing so we would blend in. But it soon dawned on us that we might be putting them at risk by accepting their hospitality. Three days passed and we put our heads together and decided it would be better for the locals, if we roughed it in the dense woods surrounding the village. We took blankets, and anything else we thought might be useful, from our abandoned camp. The villagers, to their credit, pleaded with us to take shelter with them, fearing the weather would turn and we would struggle to survive out of doors.

We compromised and slept in the woods, only returning to Marengo for food and water. As I tried to find sleep each night, I was comforted by the sweet smell of the leaves and the stillness of the dense woodland, even though I knew the weather was changing, the morning and evening air now cooling my face and hands. I would often lay waiting for sleep to engulf me, appreciating how wonderfully kind the villagers had been to us, we after all were the enemy and they'd treated us like family.

We camped on the edge of the village for five more days, until we received definite word the Germans were sweeping through the villages in our immediate vicinity, in search of escaped prisoners. The net was closing in on us and Ted and I discussed the options we had and came to the conclusion we had to make a move, yet our two companions had gone to the village the previous day and hadn't returned.

We didn't know what to do.

The villagers sent a small boy to warn us our comrades had been forced to flee in the opposite direction when a German patrol turned up unexpectedly. It was then that we put our plan into action. Ted and I would attempt to head north in the direction of the Swiss border, estimating we were somewhere in the region of one hundred and seventy miles from freedom.

Anne and the family could know nothing of the risk Ted and I were prepared to make in our bid to be free. Little did we realise that the Allies would take Naples on 1st October and Italy herself would declare war on Germany on October 13th.

My head felt as though it was held in a vice. In our attempt to remain free, living and breathing men, we were putting our lives at risk once more. I prayed somebody up on high was looking out for two dishevelled men on the run.

10

It was September 15th 1943 when we made our break for it. The villagers packed bread, cheese and fruit for us and we carried water in goat skins we fixed to our backs. The village elders took us through a path in the woods that was known only to them and as we made our way slowly into the forest, the trees seemed to draw closer together and only occasional light broke through.

Autumn had arrived and many of the leaves on the trees were turning brown, but thankfully there was sufficient cover to hide us from potential pursuers. Had our escape been planned a month or so later, Ted's bulky frame would have been spotted for miles around.

I remember feeling the bite of cold in the permanent shade of those trees and knew that, had our guides wanted us to perish, they would only have needed to abandon us right where we stood. Large sections of the forest were bathed in permanent darkness and without expert knowledge we would never have found our way out.

We reached an abrupt end when the trees simply vanished and found ourselves looking into a meadow that had been left fallow, sporting high untidy grasses, giving us excellent cover as luck would have it. Our friends from the village hugged us and wished us well, each man crossing himself, denoting their belief in the power of Catholicism.

"God bless both of you," a village elder said to us, his blue eyes shining within a face that was as brown and wrinkled as an old paper bag.

We left them behind and followed the path they suggested, praying it would lead us to a succession of villages and ultimately freedom.

*

After more than a day's walk, we reached the next village who had somehow received word we were on our way. They had no hesitation in offering us food for immediate consumption and provisions for the next part of our journey.

We must have looked a sight, unshaven and unkempt, and we didn't smell too sweetly either, but this was overlooked by these consistently kind and empathetic people.

We took our food and water into the relative safety of the forest and stopped near a tributary that was no more than a trickle really, but I announced I was going no further without washing myself down. Ted stood guard as I stripped and found the soap we'd confiscated from San Bernadino.

I was half way through my routine when Ted spoke softly.

"Did you hear something Gus?"

I stopped what I was doing and strained with all my might to listen. I was just about to chastise him for being stupid, when I heard the sound of footsteps and muffled voices.

"I heard that. Quick get down," I instructed him, feeling for my underclothing.

My heart was beating so fast I thought it was going to burst, but I dared not speak, my eyes hungrily surveying the area we had come from. Then from nowhere, a short man wearing a long grey overcoat worn by German Officers, walked into the clearing and stopped with his back to us. He reached for something in his pocket and I looked across at Ted and we shrugged at each other, our faces displaying fear and confusion. What should we do? Do we jump him and risk him calling to his comrades? Or do we stay out of sight?

He lit up a cigarette and the smoke from it reached our noses and I must say that despite our situation I longed for a drag on it. We kept low, but part of my kit and provisions were strewn near the stream and as the man's head turned in our direction, he made our mind up for us. We nodded to each other and pounced on him.

It was no easy feat, even though we taken him by surprise, the man was powerful. But Ted was still as strong as an ox and wrestled him to the ground. Ted's big hand covered his lower face and as I reached for a stout branch with which to silence him, I looked again at the prone figure struggling to tell us something, when I quickly realised what he was trying to say.

I stood.

"What are you doing Gus?"

"Let him up Ted and take a good look. This is no Jerry."

He let the man go and squinted at the hairy, dirty looking man.

"I don't believe it," Ted said.

"Jimmy Kite as I live and breathe," I added.

"Gus why in God's name are you standin' in the forest in yer' birthday suit?" was all Jimmy said, as the three of us broke into fits of laughter.

11

Once I was properly dressed, Jimmy explained that he was also trying to find his way to the Swiss border in the company of three men he'd escaped with. He retraced his steps and brought them to where Ted and I waited and it was agreed we'd join up. We found a clearing deep in the forest and huddled together and exchanged experiences and provisions.

We learned that Jimmy had also been injured during our final battle, but although his wounds had not been serious, he'd been rendered unconscious and was rounded up long after we had departed. His story was a similar one to ours. The conditions of the camps he frequented were rough and many men died, but as Ted and I did, he worked in the fields up until he was declared a free man.

He was pretty cut up about Floppy when I gave him the news. He'd always harboured a real soft spot for the lad.

As a group we made our way to two more villages, taking what they could spare us, but still sleeping in the woods. This pattern continued until we reached a village called Merella. There we were befriended by an Italian known only to us as Gio. His heavy black beard and his peasant's clothing did little to give us confidence in him. The Germans would surely pay him to turn us in. I listened as he explained in perfect English that it was presently too dangerous to make it for the border. He explained we'd been outflanked by the German army, who were positioned between Merella and the border and how they'd already picked up hundreds of men. He offered us shelter in a safe house in the hills outside the village and promised to bring us food and news of German movements when he could.

We had no alternative other than to sit tight and put our trust in a man we hardly knew, a man who could have been a collaborator for all we knew. At least we'd stay warm and dry as we waited.

I experienced a combination of anger and frustration. We'd come so far and were so close to freedom, only to find that the final leg of our escape route was riddled with German soldiers. Paranoia also began to take effect and I started to question the motives of those about me. How well did we know Gio? Surely he must be collaborator, I told myself. Were we sitting ducks waiting in his house? And were the Germans really swarming all over the Swiss border routes?

Fortunately I didn't share any of my concerns with the others which was just as well.

For five days we stayed hidden and each day as promised Gio brought us food.

But on the fifth day when he came, he was agitated. He called us together explaining that his sources had passed him word, that German troops were closing in on the area and that we would be best advised to move to the next village. He assured us the locals would do everything to assist us, but the enemy had grown wise to the policy of prisoners of war making for Swiss border and we would need to be careful and cunning to avoid capture.

We thanked him and took the food and water he'd prepared for us and, as we left, another thought entered my head. We'd need luck on our side more than ever, if our bid for escape was to succeed.

*

We reached the next village close to nightfall and slept in the woods until dawn. One of us was always on watch and this was how we discovered there were others like us in the forest. I stopped two men who were looking for a place to rest, without any food or water. There were other similar cases, totalling eight men in all and suddenly our motley band had grown to twelve men and while you might think there'd be safety in numbers, so many men brought a different set of problems entirely. Could we gather enough food to feed all twelve? And how could we expect to move unnoticed in a group of this size?

12

Rumours of troop movements reached the many ears of our small group thanks to the villagers, who continued to help us and we came to the conclusion it might be prudent to act quickly, if we were to avoid capture.

Jimmy was put in touch with an Italian soldier, who agreed to guide us through the mountains in return for everything we had, including the ragged clothing on our backs. We didn't know what to do after hearing stories about Italians taking men for all they had, then handing them over to the Germans for a fee. The stories told of allied soldiers losing their lives by firing squad and we didn't want to be left rotting in shallow graves, when we were so close to freedom. But could we trust this Italian Jimmy had made contact with?

After a cold and sleepless night, we heard machine gun fire that sounded far too close for comfort and our minds were made up. Jimmy arranged it and we set off at dusk to meet our fate.

We met the rail-thin man, sporting a grubby uniform and five o'clock shadow. He took all of our cigarettes and an assortment of personal belongings, such as watches and rings. One man even gave our guide a silver snuff box, that had been in his family for generations, but that was how desperate we were.

I tried not to judge the soldier, after all he was risking his life helping us and why should he not be rewarded?

We followed him for six days through mountainous terrain, starving and half scared to death, but to our collective relief, the anticipated interception by the German army did not materialise. Perhaps we'd been lucky, but I prefer to think our guide, who was a local man, knew his stuff. The journey we traversed was interspersed with sheer drops and seemingly unsurpassable peaks, yet we all made it, with no more than a few cuts and bruises. I was thankful for our time on the farm that had helped us return to the best possible condition, but when we finally reached the Swiss border on 30th September 1943, in only our underclothing, we were a rag tag band. There were different degrees of course, but each of us was much the worse for the experience.

Our guide bid us goodbye, leaving us within touching distance of freedom.

The Swiss National Guard met us at the border and supplied us with a coarse blanket each and a little food and water, from their rations. They allowed us to rest before we embarked on a five mile march to a Swiss village. There we were given some bread and cheese, and each of us enjoyed a good night's sleep for the first time in what seemed a very long time. Next morning, quite refreshed, we marched to another village where we were again fed and watered.

A bus then took us to another small town and after another feed we were ushered aboard a train that took us to a hotel. At the hotel we were able to take a bath and were given temporary clothing. Then we were treated to the best meal any of us had enjoyed for many a year. There were what our hosts described as Rosti potatoes, consisting of layers of grated potato and cheese. I'd never tasted it before, it was absolutely delicious, but then again anything they'd served us would have been. With the rosti potatoes we were given veal and an unpronounceable white bread the locals called zupfe. Accompanying the meal was a ration of schnapps for each man and after many years of abstinence the alcohol went straight to our heads. We then slept like a company of infants in real beds with clean sheets. After my finest night's sleep in years, we were all taken to a place called Visp, a small place known for very little other than skiing by the locals. There we were reunited with our own kind and fitted for battle dress, complete with toilet kit.

Feeling and looking like British soldiers again we were taken to a camp, where there were nearly five hundred men and the camp was run by our own officers.

There we received our full rate of pay.

*

I was overjoyed. I was a free man again. On top of this I had made it under my own steam and with the kinship of two of the closest friends a man can have. But little did I realise at the time, that I would wait almost fourteen months before seeing my family again.

Emily in a portrait she had taken for her sons in postcard form

Anne's Story - part 4

1

We stayed with Mrs Lea until May of 1944. By this time the war was swinging in our favour and the word was that it was safe for most evacuees to return to their homes, but for me there was an added incentive to return to Liverpool. We learned Angus had escaped into Switzerland and I assumed it was only a matter of time before he was shipped back home.

I would miss the friends I'd made and the green fields and clean air was something the children and I would both lose out on, but the prospect of welcoming Angus home was my overriding impulse and everything else seemed secondary in my mind. I wanted to return to my old life with all haste to prepare for his return, no matter how long it would take for them to send him back to me.

The Russians had begun to turn the tide on the German occupation in Autumn of 1943 and by January of 1944 they had advanced into Poland. Peter was with the Allies in Italy during this period, the land war in North Africa having been won.

Through March and April of 1944, Berlin was subjected to constant bombing raids and although I was happy we'd at last gained the upper hand, I spared a thought for the ordinary German people. They were experiencing what we'd suffered during May of 1941 in Liverpool and this brought nothing but death, destruction and heartache.

*

We said our goodbyes and took the reverse route home, by bus and train. Somehow the journey back didn't seem as long, although I knew it must have been. I supposed it only felt shorter because we were returning to the place we belonged. James and Emily were looking forward to seeing their Grandparents again, although for Rhona, who was now three, it was a virtual journey into the unknown and I worried how she might react to her new surroundings. After all, she'd only been a babe in arms when we left Harrogate Street.

There were still sand bags strewn about the bombed out streets and barrage balloons could still be seen swaying on the skyline, although bombing raids on Liverpool seemed unlikely. I thought the Germans had enough on their plate. Despite the obvious signs of war, spring was in the air and the trees were filled with new leaves and daffodils and tulips were in bloom everywhere in the parks. What a wonderful sight it was. It might have been my imagination, but I felt that the people of Liverpool had a confident air about them. There certainly seemed to be more smiles on the faces of strangers on the street, as the tram chugged on towards our final destination. Like me, I knew my fellow Liverpudlians wanted to see the end of war, we'd all had a belly full of it. Perhaps like me they sensed the end was in sight and more importantly, it looked as if we would be the victors and that was certainly something to cheer about. It hardly seemed possible in the early days when Hitler's war machine crushed everything in its path, when only Britain and a handful of her allies stood in his way.

I now dared to look forward to a life beyond a war that had held our future in its stranglehold for far too long.

2

    I hadn't warned old Groves of our impending return, nor had I made contact with Angus's parents once I'd decided to come home. You have to remember, the only way to do so in those days would have been by sending a telegram and this tended to be reserved for emergencies only. I certainly didn't want to alarm anybody, so I booked our return journey back and told James and Emily it would be a big surprise for Nana and both Granddads. They both liked the idea and chattered and giggled about the possible expressions on the faces of Emily, James and old Groves, when they clapped eyes on us. This at least gave them something to think about during the long journey home.

    It was late afternoon when we arrived in Harrogate Street and as we walked into the narrow space of terraced houses facing each other, separated by a narrow strip of cobbles, the place somehow seemed to have shrunk. It was clear that the wide open spaces we'd been recently used to had affected my view of the place, but it hadn't erased the memories. My eyes filled up as I walked to my home and recalled my early life with William and Eleanor Groves and the trials and tribulations I put them through, particularly during my school days and the truancy that was a big part of it. I recalled the visits of my eldest sister Fanny, who made it her business to visit me every week without fail, because of a promise she had made to God himself, following the death of our Mother all those years before. I still could see the pain on the face of my eldest brother John, the day he came to take me to view the corpse of an uncle I'd never laid eyes on in life. Then the feelings of worthlessness that coursed through me once John had told me the awful truth. I then remembered a certain Bonfire Night in 1929 and the light from the fire that danced in the smiling eyes of the man I would marry. Then there was our marriage and the birth of our children.

    My whole life had been spent in this place and as I fought back the tears I realised how relieved I was to be home again.

*

    Old Groves was at work and although we stopped to speak with some old neighbours, we continued on up to Rishton Street and knocked on Emily's door. I was beginning to think she was out at the shops when the door finally opened and the imposing figure of Emily Brown looked down upon us from a spotless front step. It was intriguing to see her expressionless face alter as her brain registered what her eyes could see. She smiled warmly and I was surprised to note that her eyes filled up, as she scooped James and Emily into her arms and led us all into her home. Once inside she took our coats and threw her arms around me. I was quite taken aback by this show of emotion and hoped my face didn't betray the surprise.

"Oh Anne, why didn't you warn us that you were coming back? We would have met you at the station."

"We wanted to surprise you Nana," little Emily piped up and then proceeded to have a fit of the giggles.

"Well you certainly did that. And just look at the three of you," she announced, fixing her eyes on the children, "you're all so big now."

James and Emily beamed back at her, but Rhona clung to me, clearly wondering who this strange woman was.

"Let me put the kettle on Anne and fetch the children a drink too, you must all be parched," she said, then shouting over the noise of the water filing up the kettle she went on. "I want to hear all about Mrs Lea and what you've been up to."

3

We talked long into the afternoon, about Mrs Lea, her good friend Mrs Woodcock and old Tom and his homemadewines. The only interruptions occurred when Emily had to check on the stew she was cooking, under a slow light on the stove. The children were playing outside and Rhona had gradually warmed to Emily and was now happily sitting on her Grandmother's knee.

There was a commotion at the front door and in walked Angus's Father, wearing a flat cap and clutching James and Emily to his breast.

"Look what I found in the street," he quipped in his thick Scottish brogue, "two 'a the finest jewels a man could ever want." He then planted a kiss on the head of each child and released them.

"And who's this bonny lass?" he went on, his eye catching little Rhona, who to my great surprise smiled back at her Grandfather and held out her little arms to him, happily allowing him to pick her up.

He then came around and kissed me on the cheek.

"You're looking well Anne. The country air obviously agrees with you all. You'll stay for tea won't you?"

"It's already organised," Emily said. "You go and wash up James and then collect William."

James must have noted the look on my face.

"Aye lass. William has been having his meals with us these past years and he's in fine fettle I can tell you. Let me get sorted and I'll walk 'round and fetch him."

"If it's alright I'd like to, I mean as long as it's okay?"

"Of course it is love," said Emily, "my two big grandchildren can help me set the table while you do that. But don't be too long love, the potatoes are almost done."

I grabbed my coat and rushed back down to Harrogate Street, hoping I wouldn't meet any of my old neighbours on the way. I wanted to surprise Groves and didn't want anyone giving the game away. As I approached his door the street was deserted, which was usually the case as most of the residents ate their evening meals at the same time and I was pleased about this.

I pushed at the door and was not surprised to find it on the latch. In those days hardly anybody locked their doors, because there was always a neighbour to watch over your home. Even now

I knew there were probably several pairs of eyes watching me approach my childhood home.

"Is that you James?" his voice boomed out and although my heart skipped a beat at the sound of it, I held my tongue and rushed inside.

He was nowhere to be seen. He'd obviously slipped into the kitchen, but then called out.

"Just coming."

He ambled into the sitting room, fiddling with the middle button on his jacket, but when he looked up, his jaw dropped open and he stopped dead in his tracks.

"My God girl, you could give an old man a fright sneaking around like that."

He looked stunned, bemused mostly and also in that split second he looked much older than I'd remembered.

"Come 'ere you silly old bugger and give your daughter an 'ug."

And he did.

I held him close and although he'd always been a slim man, there seemed to be less of him.

I turned his face to mine and wiped the tears from his eyes with my hankie.

"Ave you been eatin' enough old man?" I asked.

"I do alright. Don't you worry about me. In fact I 'aven't felt this good in years. But seeing you fit and healthy is a proper tonic for me, make no mistake about that my girl."

"Come on then, let's reintroduce you to your grandchildren," I said, and we finally stood apart, but I soon linked his arm as we made our way into the street.

4

It was good to be back at my own place and once I'd put fresh sheets on the beds and cleaned each room thoroughly, it felt like home again. I soon slipped back into my old routine; of cleaning, cooking and everything else that came with Motherhood, while I waited for any news of Angus's return home.

It was to be a long wait and during the time that elapsed, the war continued to swing in our favour. Even so, there were still to be many thousands of casualties as the final battle lines were drawn in Europe. In June the allies took Rome and this was also the month of the D-Day landings. The ring was closing in around Hitler, but in July yet another assassination attempt failed, the monster seemed to be impossible to kill.

In August the Polish home army organised an uprising against the Nazis and were swiftly aided and abetted by the Russians, who began liberating concentration camps. The first was Majdenek, not too far from the Russian border and this was when the first news of mass genocide began to circulate. There had always been rumours of such things but never any proof. In fact, it was later established that over 230,000 people lost their lives at Majdenek, over 100,000 of them Jews. When the horrific reality of it sank in and other camps were liberated, I felt genuinely ashamed to call myself a member of the human race.

The Polish uprising continued on into August of 1944 when they fought for control of Warsaw, but the Germans were far from finished and launched a series of counter attacks. Paris was liberated on the 25th August and this gave everyone in Britain a massive lift, to learn that one of our closest allies was at last free. This also enabled the French army to assist in the next push as the Allies targeted Germany herself.

Around this time I received a brief note from the war office to confirm that Angus was to return home and I was forced to re-read the date they were sending him back to me. He was returning home Sunday, 5th November 1944. They were sending him home on bonfire night and I therefore knew it was meant to be.

I rushed to tell Emily and James and we all shed a tear or two after I'd given them my news. I was all of a twitter and it wasn't until James uncorked his malt whiskey, that was only ever opened on very special occasions, and poured me a large one, did my nerves start to calm. Little James and Emily were overjoyed and were suddenly filled with a nervous energy I'd not seen in them for months. After another snifter each, we hatched a plan to organise a party in Harrogate Street to commemorate his return and though I hadn't as yet raised the subject with our friends and neighbours, I felt certain they'd want to help.

I wasn't disappointed, but then that was how people were in those days.

That night as I put James to bed, I sensed that something was ailing him and when I questioned him about it he burst into tears. After a little more cajoling he eventually told me what it was, but wouldn't look at me while he was speaking.

"Mam, Bobby said that Dad'll have bits of 'im missing when 'e comes 'ome."

"What do you mean by bits of 'im?" I asked, the anxiety related to my son's question making my voice sound shrill. I think he thought I was angry with him.

Tears were streaming down his little face by this time, but he looked down at the candlewick bedspread and began to run his index finger along the intricate pattern.

"Like no arm or legs."

"Come 'ere you silly child. Don't you think I'd tell you if something like that 'ad 'appened?" I assured him, holding him to me and wiping the tears away with my apron.

"What about 'is brain then? Bobby says when some soldiers come 'ome after the war they go completely off their rockers."

I looked up to the ceiling truly feeling my anger rise this time.

"Wait until I see Bobby Norman," I muttered to myself, but taking a deep breath before continuing. "Look when your Father comes 'ome 'e'll need lots a rest and if he does 'ave days when he thinks about 'is pals who might 'ave died during the war, it'll probably make 'im feel sad, but with our 'elp 'e'll get over it quickly." I took his head in my hands and held his gaze, "besides, your Father's always been a little bit mad, why on earth d'ya think 'e married me?"

It was good to hear him laugh.

"Next time ask me before believin' what *Mr know ir' all* Bobby Norman tells you. Good night son."

"Good night Mam."

As I turned out the light, I was certain his sister, who was in the next bed to him, had flinched and if so she'd also heard every word. I was secretly pleased, I didn't fancy going through the same performance with her.

5

Even though I was occupied with planning our street party, the days and weeks seemed to move very slowly and November seemed a long way off.

There was good and bad news from the war during September and October, although most of it was in our favour. The Allies began an airborne assault on occupied Holland in mid September and by the 26th the Soviets occupied Estonia. In early October I was disappointed to hear that the Polish home army had surrendered to the Germans who were able to quell the brief uprising in Warsaw. I had great sympathy for the Poles and I suppose this was because, it seemed to me, they were the perpetual underdog during the war. I don't know why, but I always liked to see the no-hoper win through.

By October 14th, Athens had been taken by the Allies and Rommel took his own life; a man who lived and died honourably from what little I knew about him. Angus had often written that the war in North Africa had been led by two gentlemen, namely Monty and Rommel, and how respect was shown by each side. If this had been true about Irwin Rommel, it seemed a shame to me that another good man had died unnecessarily at the hands of Adolf Hitler.

There was more good news for the allies on October 21st when there was a mass surrender by the German army in Aachen, an area close to their borders with both Luxemburg and Belgium.

*

After what had seemed an eternity, bonfire night of 1944 finally came around. My wonderful neighbours had spent a couple of days helping me prepare the food, with the meagre rations we still had to manage on, and every house in the street was involved. Even those who could not contribute any food provided furniture and strips of material from goodness knows where to make bunting.

I recall looking back down the street to a line of tables and chairs and the array of pristine tablecloths. Union jacks were everywhere to be seen and all present wore their Sunday best. The sight of it brought tears to my eyes.

Thankfully the weather was dry.

All we needed now was my husband.

*

It was late, everyone's children apart from mine had been carted off to bed and still he hadn't shown up. I began to worry that something awful had happened to him on the last leg of his journey back to me. Darkness had fallen like a huge blackout curtain and at the far end of the street a small bonfire was still smouldering. This was a rather pathetic affair compared to the massive bommies (as we called them) we'd seen before the war. The problem was nobody had an awful lot to burn, when raw materials were terribly difficult to come by, particularly as almost all of our natural resources were fuelling the allied war machine. The other reason it was such a modest bonfire related to the nervous state of the local fire officer. To be fair to the man, his views had most definitely been coloured by the horrors of falling bombs, particularly during The Blitz. He'd witnessed firsthand the damage fire could do and we accepted his opinion without argument and kept only a small one burning on into the night.

I couldn't eat a thing and long after people had begun to return to their homes, most of the food had been eaten and Emily had taken my children inside and put them to bed, I stumbled into my own home, numb, from the cold and bitter disappointment.

Harrogate Rent Book

Angus's Story - part 4

1

It was the first time I'd ever been near an aeroplane of any kind, let alone travelling in one. But the top brass had decided that with the Germans in retreat, the risks of us meeting enemy aircraft had considerably receded. We were driven to the small airfield in cattle trucks, the picturesque snow-capped mountains all around us and the chilly air carrying biting shards of winter wind. Luckily we'd been prepared and were wearing our heavy woollen coats, hats and gloves, not to mention our warm underclothes. It was a happy ride despite the cold, mostly because we all knew we were finally on our way home.

We were asked to climb into an old B52 bomber, no longer required to do the thing she was built for, in single file. We were told to sit on the two rows of benches that had been fixed to the plane's insides. We sauntered in, spacing ourselves so that each man had a strap that was fixed to the roof above him. I assumed this was in the event of turbulence or enemy attack, although they were never referred to. A five-minute demonstration on how to open a parachute was then given to us by our NCO, before each man was instructed in no uncertain terms to wear the chute until they were told otherwise.

Our cramped surroundings smelled of sweat and fear and it was impossible to catch any man's eye. Nobody wanted to admit it, but I'm certain we were all thinking that if we were asked to face the enemy again, or take this journey, we'd all have chosen the former.

As the propellers started up, the craft began to shake violently and the noise was deafening. I couldn't imagine how this crude assortment of metal could conceivably get off the ground, let alone fly and as we waited for clearance any hope of conversation was out of the question. My mind spun backwards like the turning of the great propellers, springing into action in tune with the plane engines, remembering the journey that had brought me this far.

*

It felt to me that decades had passed; it had only been just over four years, but they were four long years. I'd seen more than most men see in a lifetime and in terms of life experiences, I felt as old as Methusla.

I thought back to my wait for my call up papers, knowing I'd done it for Anne's sake, but unable to shake the feeling it was wrong somehow, when men all around me were volunteering in their droves. But I soon cottoned on that they were not all men, some were boys. Very like Floppy, that laid back, sweet natured lad, who'd thought war was a game of valour and hadn't counted on back breaking toil, bullies and ultimately death.

He'd paid the ultimate price for his cockeyed idea of what war was all about and when I thought of him, the memory of it was still raw. I could have cried a river of tears for him there and then, but in years to come when I thought of him it was always with fondness.

I remembered the faces of my children James and Emily vividly from years before and held them close to my heart, yet I realised they might now have altered beyond all recognition. James, my brave little man, not wanting to show he was scared for me and my sweet Emily, oblivious to the fact she might not see her Father again for a very long time.

Much longer than any of us had envisaged.

Yet I was luckier than many. I was, after all, on my way home to Anne and the children in one piece, and although Rhona's features were a mystery to me, now she was no longer a babe in arms; I couldn't help but wonder who she might favour.

I thought back to the months of captivity, to the men who had lost their lives needlessly from starvation or typhoid and how lucky Ted, Jimmy and I had been. Then our dramatic journey, that took us through rural Italy and ultimately the Alps and into the sanctuary of Switzerland.

The Swiss people had been wonderful, if a little reserved. Yet this was their way, they had after all managed to ignore the death and destruction all around them, as millions died in an effort to preserve freedom. Thinking like that drove me mad at times and I therefore pushed those depressing thoughts from my mind and tried to concentrate on the positives. After all, had the Swiss chosen to fight would we have had a safe haven to escape to?

Our camp at Visp was no more than a place to sleep, even though our NCO saw to it we maintained discipline and a dress code. We all had chores to carry out and they could swiftly be taken care of after roll call, but once done the day was our own.

All of us formed friendships with the locals and I was no different. I promised myself that I'd come back to this beautiful country one day in the future, bringing Anne and my family back with me.

I experienced a certain amount of guilt for flourishing in this place and along with the majority of married men, it came as a great relief to learn they were finally sending us home.

2

The noise from the bone-shaker was deafening and she seemed to be straining every rivet before lifting off the ground, but eventually she did, leaving my stomach somewhere below.

I'd calculated the significance of my proposed date of repatriation and smiled inwardly at what the date meant to Anne and I.

Surely this was meant to be.

Little did I know then, that the fates had contrived to prolong our agony and there was to be one final twist of the knife before my trial was finally over.

*

We were hit by bad weather and because of it a lack of fuel. This meant we were forced to land at Wittering airfield near Yeovil, instead of RAF Hooton, near Birkenhead, which was much nearer to home for me and this put the kibosh on my well oiled return home. We were supposed to be given an overnight stay at the airbase and then journey home by rail the next day. The entire operation had to re-scheduled and instead of Harrogate Street and the city of my birth, I was stranded in the south the morning of 5th November 1944. After a series of rail journeys and a final lift from the home defences, I eventually stumbled onto the cobbled streets of my home at almost 4.00 am on 6th November, but as it was still dark I told myself that it was still bonfire night.

I was dog tired, but once I was in sight of home the adrenaline began pumping through my veins and I was suddenly longing to be with my family. My step quickened as I hurried to the door of number 17 Harrogate Street, a smile lighting up my face in the darkness for the first time in days.

I wrapped heavily on the door, as tears welled up in my eyes and my heart swelled up so big, that I swear I could have floated right up into the early morning sky and joined the barrage balloons.

The door creaked open and an unfamiliar face peeped out at me.

Either this little wisp of a thing was Rhona, or my family no longer resided here.

I smiled down at the pretty face and watched helplessly as her bottom lip quivered and she began to cry. Who could blame her?

I must have looked a sight. I'd travelled for days to reach my own front door.

Rhona disappeared, but a face I did recognise eventually peered up at me. Emily, virtually a babe in arms when I left, was now a fully-fledged little girl. Her eyes lit up when she saw me and suddenly all of the long years quickly evaporated.

"Daddy!" she squealed and then went on, "Daddy's home everybody!"

The tears fell from my red-rimmed eyes as I took her in my arms and carried her into the house.

Soon I felt Anne's arms encircle me and we were both crying as Rhona looked on also tearful, but for an entirely different reason.

James had not awoken amid all of the commotion and as Anne's big tear sodden eyes looked into mine, I knew I was finally home.

"Oh Angus!" was all I recall her saying.

*

I didn't go to bed for hours and Anne allowed me to tramp upstairs in my heavy boots to look in on my sleeping son. I crept into the bedroom and marvelled at his angelic form as he lay on his side, his right hand resting on his ruddy cheek and it was only as I brushed my fingers through his thick mop of hair, the waterworks began again. He eventually stirred and rubbed his eyes to make sure what he was seeing was real and once satisfied, he pulled himself into a sitting position and threw himself into my arms.

He smelled delicious, the way only children can and we stayed that way for a long time, neither of us wanting to let go.

After disengaging, he carefully looked me all over and then smiled broadly at my puzzled expression.

"Bobby was wrong."

"About what son?" I asked laughing, reaching out and mussing his hair again.

"Oh it doesn't matter," he told me, "just as long as you're 'ere."

He then embraced me again much tighter this time, burying his face into my chest to try and hide the hot tears running from his own eyes.

We joined the others downstairs and with the exception of Rhona, who'd fallen asleep in front of the fire, we all enjoyed a cup of *Ovaltine* as I told them all about the snow in Switzerland and my incredible journey home.

*

I was granted leave on full pay until 18th December, although this was eventually extended until 28th December, but I was told off the record that as the war was expected to be over in a matter of months, I was unlikely to see action again.

*

After a few hours of sleep I washed and shaved and put on my best suit, though it seemed to hang off my shrunken frame, and made my way up to Rishton Street. Father cried and Mother was close to it. Margie and Albert called on us later and I caught up on the news about Johnny, Peter and Tommy Davies, who all were still at war.

People were still dying, but it was over for me, yet I couldn't truly relax until V. E. day. I did some driving for the home guard and some administrative work for my own regiment right up until December of 1945, until I was finally discharged on 12th March 1946 after what had been classed as 99 days leave. They told me I was eligible for call up again until the age of forty-five, although I didn't think it was likely.

As far as I was concerned the war was over for good and our lives could begin again. We were free and all I could see ahead of me was the good life and I intended to enjoy every minute of it.

Margie's Story

1

My Mother, was at times, a difficult woman to know and this was undoubtedly as a direct result of her Victorian upbringing. Behaving properly was at the core of Victorian society and this had been drummed into a young Emily Coffee from a very early age. And even though she raised us in a working class environment, she instilled in us all of her values. To some of our neighbours, we were perhaps perceived as snooty and some of them I know assumed we considered ourselves superior, but that was far from the truth. Our upbringing and ideals were much more complex than that. We were taught good manners and expected to act with a certain decorum, but this was no reflection on our friends and neighbours, it was simply all that Mother knew.

It is true that I didn't always condone her every action and I refer to her refusal to attend the wedding of Angus and Anne as a prime example, but who reading this can claim to have no faults? To add to this, my Mother never claimed to be perfect. Therefore, as she is unable to answer for herself, I feel I must at the very least present my Mother's conduct from another viewpoint, by shedding a little more light on her early life.

She hailed from a middle class background and although she was more privileged than many of her fellow Liverpudlians, she had known suffering. Her Father died in an accident on the railway when she was only a girl and her Mother, who struggled to recover from her loss, became somewhat distant from her daughter. I think this is where my Mother's great strength of character first sprouted wings. Her own Mother suffered both financially and emotionally and Emily Coffee found herself making many of her Mother's decisions and her resourcefulness during this period of her life was to shape her character.

True enough, my Mother was bombastic and portentous at times. And you could add that she always believed strongly in the strength of her convictions and was known to be extremely stubborn when the mood took her. Yet before you judge her too harshly, show me a Mother who doesn't want the best for her offspring. It was true she did not approve of Anne when they were first introduced, but believe me when I say this was nothing personal. I know for certain she admired Anne's spirit and strength once she got to know her better. As only a parent can truly understand, my Mother simply wanted the best for each of her children and if their chosen partner did not match up to her own expectations, she found it hard to totally accept that individual.

My abiding memory of my Mother is of a woman who was prepared to stand or fall by beliefs. I also remember she was very particular about her appearance and never left the house without looking her very best.

Some say I favour her in looks, even though she was much taller than I ever became.

Rightly or wrongly I've always considered this the highest compliment possible.

Father was the polar opposite to my Mother, yet they made a surprisingly good team and I'm certain they loved each with the same intensity as my dear Albert and I, which is saying something.

James 'Jock' Brown's Mother was a Mackenzie, hence the continuation of the name. He was born at 37 Oakhill Street, Tillacoutry, Sterling, in November of 1878 and moved to Liverpool as a young man to take an apprenticeship with the Mersey Docks and Harbour Board, as a Cooper and went onto earn the prestigious title of Master Cooper. This is a skill now virtually extinct in Britain, but suffice to say my Father was an expert barrel or cask maker.

He was a man who wore his heart on his sleeve and easily displayed his emotions. On top of that he was extremely easy going and would often bring wild flowers home that he'd picked on his way home from work. He also had a shed in the back yard in which he collected bits of old lead he would sell on and any commodity he believed he could use to good effect. He was very good with his hands and would often repair our shoes with bits of old leather he'd acquire somehow.

My Mother without doubt married beneath her class, but I'm certain she didn't regret a single day she had with my Father.

I often think about the war years and marvel at the will of the working classes. Parents sent their boys to war and held their emotions inside. My parents had immense strength and although they experienced the terrible pain of losing a child before the conflict, they were luckier than most during wartime, welcoming Johnny, Angus and Peter back home. My parents were survivors and lived long enough to enjoy much of the post war prosperity.

To my mind, nobody deserved it more.

2

My brother James Mackenzie Brown was born in 1905 and died in July of 1932. Mother and Father were mortally wounded as the result of his untimely death.

My vague memories of him are sketchy. I remember that Anne's eldest son James, who became Jim in adulthood; favoured his namesake, although thankfully not my brother's nature. He was certainly a good-looking specimen, yet I must say he was difficult to like.

Some say it is wrong to speak ill of the dead, yet in all honesty I must go on record to say my eldest brother thought he was a cut above everyone else. Quite why he should think that way I've never understood.

I was only twelve when he died, but I can think of nothing that endeared him to me and it saddens me to say so.

Nevertheless as I've already said, my parents were devastated by his death, but never once did they dare to discuss the subject of his demise in public, clearly for fear of how they might react.

*

John McIntosh Brown was born in 1907.

I didn't always see eye to eye with my next eldest brother, although this perhaps related to our disparity in age.

Johnny or Jack was a highly strung individual. It was therefore no surprise when he suffered a nervous breakdown at the age of twenty. His employers at the time were the Adelphi Hotel. They sent him to a sanatorium in Benfleet, Essex, where I'm pleased to announce he made a full recovery. I always thought well of them for taking him back and even promoting him in later years.

Johnny was very close to Mother. He liked to dress well and as a young man suffered from a similar trait to our brother James and sometimes gave the impression he was a cut above the rest of us. As I've said we were never close when young, but I'm happy to tell you as we both matured and the years passed, our relationship improved and we became much closer.

*

Peter McIntosh Brown was born in 1911 and tormented me daily from the day I was old enough to communicate. He took pleasure in playing tricks on me and was always full of fun. He was the tallest of my brothers at just under six foot. He had dark hair like all of us and was blessed with a rather prominent nose.

Peter could also play the piano by ear, something which, even to this day, I find fascinating. He would often find a piano when we were socialising as adults and strike up the tune of the day without rehearsal.

He was another fun-loving person, but was most unlucky to marry a woman like Elsie Flowers, who ultimately cheated on him.

He deserved better.

Angus and Peter were very close and complimented each other perfectly.

If there is a heaven I expect they are both up there somewhere on pure merit, still playing pranks on each other and making all around them laugh with their infectious personalities.

*

Albert Vernon Smedley was born 8/3/21 in Liverpool. He was working as an apprentice to a local butcher near where I worked and from the very first moment we met, his good nature shone through. Albert was somebody who loved life and by spending any time with him, people found this contagious and as a consequence, nobody had anything but good things to say about him. He was courteous and kind to everyone he ever met and a more affectionate man you could never meet. It was my great fortune and pleasure to share my life with him and I truly believe by knowing him, my own outlook on life altered for the better.

He was of average height, with permanently ruddy cheeks and dark brown hair, but I suppose to everyone except me, he was nothing exceptional to look at.

Albert was always of the opinion that human life mirrored nature and thought that in many ways people were like plants, in that the stronger survived longer and I've often felt there was something to that theory.

3

Angus Mackenzie Brown was born in December of 1909 and he couldn't have been more different than his older brother James. He resembled Johnny physically, but again his personality was quite different, much closer to Peter's I would say.

Despite an eleven-year difference, Angus and I got along like a house on fire and even though I knew James would constantly try and belittle him, Angus would shrug it off and even go out of his way to be pleasant to his eldest brother.

I remember Angus always seemed to be in hurry. It seemed to me he loved life so much, he couldn't wait to get on with the next bit of it. He was a social animal and during pre and post war, drank his fare share of beer and smoked plenty of cigarettes, although everybody did in those days. He was shorter than Johnny and Peter in stature, but remained rake-thin all of his life.

He hardly ever talked about his experiences during the war and I never pressed him on it. I assumed it was a door he wanted to keep firmly closed and respected this.

Despite his gregarious personality, he too retained some of Mother's values and he expected his own children to behave properly. They would need to ask permission before they could leave the table during meal times and this was right out of the Emily Coffee manual on parenting.

His only other vice was reading. He loved magazines and novels of any kind and would often recommend certain authors, specific books or articles to me.

In spite of his life experiences, he was a more generous and fun-loving person you could ever hope to meet.

*

Anne was a striking young woman and when I first laid eyes on her, it was clear a fire burned behind her eyes; even though I was to quickly learn she possessed a kind heart and gentle nature. I witnessed the fire first hand on a couple of occasions, and when she lost her temper it was a sight to behold. Peter famously called her Dagger and she was certainly cutting and difficult to handle whenever the red mist descended.

She loved my brother with the same intensity and was occasionally overwhelmed by jealousy any time a member of the opposite sex showed even the slightest interest in him. This could be a problem because of my brother's propensity to socialise. There was never anything in it though, as he was devoted to her and as a result she sometimes found herself on the wrong end of a scolding from him.

In her favour she was a wonderful Mother, a famously good cook and always kept a clean house.

She and I always got on well and I had great admiration for her strength and determination. Anne's life started in the worst possible way, but she was lucky to have been rescued by Mr and Mrs Groves. It must have been hard to accept when faced with the realisation her Father abandoned the family after her birth and never once tried to know her. This I feel spurred her on and as time elapsed she grew to love her surrogate Father William Groves, with the same affection and love only a daughter can.

*

They are all gone now and I suppose if Albert was here he would tell me the strongest survive the longest and maybe that is true, but that doesn't stop me missing all of them; my parents, my brothers and of course Angus and Anne. But I miss none more than Albert.

On a positive note we all survived the war and enjoyed the prosperity that followed. As I've often said, we were much luckier than most and we certainly knew it.

Albert and Margie on their wedding day

Emily's Story

1

Whenever I look in the mirror these days I see my Mother's face, even though we're much different across the eyes. Yet if I smile I can see my Father's face and this comforts me to know that something of them lives on in me, my own children and even my grandchildren.

*

The night my Father came home to us is still vivid in my memory. In my mind's eye I can see him standing in front of me, Rhona having run off crying. But I can still recall the joy I felt, seeing him after such a long absence, though I was only five years of age at the time.

I remember Mrs Lea, plus bits and pieces related to our time in Wigan during our evacuation, but before that only snatches of things. Like, for example, my Grandmother's knitted clothing and Grandfather James in his flat cap, underneath which there always seemed to be a twinkle in his eye. I also remember William Groves' serious expression and in contrast his gentleness, despite the size and strength of his callused hands. I recall my Mother's infrequent, but undeniably violent, temper and learned very quickly that it was advisable to make a run for it once she'd lost the plot, before something, really anything, might come flying my way. She once threw half a pound of post-war butter at me, connecting with me smack on the nose, but it caused me no more than a nose bleed.

I must say, she was wracked with guilt and remorse for weeks afterward and although this would be undoubtedly classed as abuse in today's politically correct society, but I probably did plenty to rouse my Mother's anger.

After the war, rationing continued until 1954, but I only remember the laughter and the joy that was in our house, as we milked the essence of post-war prosperity, at least in spirit. My parents were so obviously in love and clearly had plenty of catching up to do and this feeling seemed to permeate through our entire lives. Clearly for my Father it was a joy to simply walk down the street and I recall how he'd take me in his arms and just hold me for no reason at all and I know he did the same with James and

Rhona. This was contagious and transcended our lives during that period.

I was an undeniable tomboy and loved to join in whatever games my brother and his friends might be playing, but even though his best friend Bobby Norman was happy to accept me, he wouldn't. But after all, what boy wants his sister stealing his thunder? And I was rather good at sports.

Yet it ran much deeper than this.

For some reason every one of my siblings has this incredible will to compete or out do the other. I was not excluded from this trait myself. Quite where this came from I do not know, but it is something that continued on into adulthood. At times it has caused extreme consternation, when coupled with the fact that each of us wore our hearts on our sleeves, much like our paternal Grandfather. There was also a temper or two amongst us: something we most definitely inherited from our mother.

2

    My Father was guilty of a similar failing to those of his Mother, never seemingly able to approve of our chosen partners when we were adults. For my part, he did not take to the man who was to become my eventual husband for a long time. Though, in many ways, my husband, like Anne, was from the wrong side of the tracks, my father couldn't see the obvious parallel to his own situation.

    As I grew to adulthood my Father and I were always close. Our love of literature gave us some common ground and even though as a girl he chastised me for trying to read passages from his adult reading material, we later ended up swapping and recommending books to each other. I have to say that my Father lived by a strict code. He was always immaculately turned out and would not stay in mixed company if a comedian used foul or abusive language when women were present. He would just pick himself up and leave the room. I shudder to imagine how he might react to today's much more liberal social life.

    I always found him easy to talk to, yet I felt there was always a bit of himself he kept from us and in my eyes at least, I have this picture of him as the consummate gentleman. He had an innate dignity that was there for all to see.

    He hardly ever mentioned his experiences during the war to us and as life enfolded and time moved on, we lost the desire to press him to talk about his remarkable experiences. Only when he was terminally ill with lung cancer he made the decision to tell parts of his story to my son and I've often wondered what prompted him to open up this way to his eldest grandson.

    My Mother and I were as close as any daughter and Mother ought to be. When I was working full time, my mother played a major role in raising my two sons; collecting them from school and caring for them until I came home. I am forever grateful to her for treating my two boys just like her own. My Mother had two massive soft spots and they certainly were not occupied by me or my sister Rhona, it perhaps explains why she doted on my own sons so much.

*

On 31ST August 1946, the final piece in our family jigsaw was complete, when Mother gave birth to her second son, who was named after his Father; Angus Mackenzie Brown. This merely underlined my parents' happiness and was a great expression of their love for each other. Although he never treated any of us differently, my Mother wasn't able to help herself. The two soft spots to which I refer, are of course my brother James, who by this time had become Jim and his much younger sibling Angus.

Angus was a dynamo from the day he was born and seemed filled with boundless energy. I remember being extremely protective of him when he was a child, I suppose because I was so much older than him. Yet as we all grew into adulthood, the age difference seemed to dissolve and in a strange way, my youngest brother at times seemed wise beyond his years. If there was ever a problem, he could always be counted upon to offer his help and support, to him blood was thicker than water.

His philosophy of casting his bread upon the water worked for him and he was as lucky in love and became a very successful local businessman, with the help of Brenda, the undoubted love of his life. Regretfully his life was tragically cut short, but his legacy and memory still burns brightly, as he left an indelible mark on anybody who had the good fortune to know him can attest.

*

In a fitting way, I must end my story by paying tribute to the two people who gave me life and much more besides. If I was a more religious person I might imagine them in paradise together, my Father dressed in his best suit, with a good book in his hand and a pint of mild at his side. My Mother would be cooking him a meal and taking occasionally sneaky peeks at the late edition of the *Liverpool Echo*, with a handful of hard-boiled sweets in her apron pocket and one in her mouth.

Wherever they are now I'm sure they'd be more than a little amused to find their story in print, in fact if I listen very carefully I can hear their contagious laughter flying to me along the airwaves.

Yes, they'd find it very entertaining indeed.

Goodnight Mum, goodnight Dad.

God bless.

The Children post-war (James top left, Emily top right, Rhona and Angus)

Acknowledgements

I first heard stories about my Grandmother's early life discussed at family gatherings, or around the dinner table when I was just a small boy, but it wasn't until my Grandfather elected to share his war stories with me that a genuine spark was ignited. He knew he was dying of terminal lung cancer and his own children were astonished he chose to share his experiences with his eldest grandson, when he'd previously never mentioned a word of his remarkable life during the war to anyone in the family.

Long after his death, a diary he kept during the war surfaced and this only added to fan the flames of curiosity. By this time I knew I wanted to write and, most of all, I knew I must tell my grandparents' story. But where would I start? There were so many gaps in the story as I knew it then and I was faced with painstaking research, particularly in regard to my Grandmother's family tree.

Their story is finally written and I hope you enjoyed it, but I feel I must thank a number of people for their invaluable assistance. Without them, this book would never have seen the light of day. Firstly I'd like to acknowledge the help I received from the staff at Liverpool Central Library when looking at Parish records and reams of microfiche, in an attempt to track down my Grandmother's family. I must also thank my Mother Emily for her unstinting support and for providing most of the photographs contained within the book. Last of all I must recognise the priceless contribution from my great aunt Margie and great uncle Albert. Without them I simply would never have written this book. They filled in so many gaps for me and joined up many of the dots, and their unselfish willingness to help in whatever way they could was typical of two remarkable people. They don't make them like Margie and Albert anymore and, perhaps it's an overused expression, but they certainly broke the mould when they came along.

Finally I must recognise the incredible contribution of my talented daughter Lucy, who not only designed the front and rear covers, but also updated my website and advised me in a myriad of ways too numerous to mention.

About the Author

Mackenzie Brown was born and raised in Liverpool, UK, where he lives with his wife, two daughters and pet cat. Having six published novels already under his belt, Brown is planning to write a sequel to his acclaimed debut novel **The Shifting,** continuing his series of detective stories set in 1940s Liverpool, featuring Vic Prince. Mackenzie Brown's inspiration for writing was borne out of wartime stories shared with him by his Grandfather and personal hero, Angus Mackenzie Brown.

You can connect with Mackenzie Brown at the following locations;

His website - http://mackbrown.weebly.com/index.html

Twitter - https://twitter.com/mackbrownbooks

Facebook - https://www.facebook.com/MackBrownBooks

His blog - http://mackenzie-brown.tumblr.com/

LinkedIn - http://www.linkedin.com/pub/mackenzie-brown/48/579/72b

Goodreads Book Club - http://www.goodreads.com/author/show/6434456.Mackenzie_Brown

Pinterest - http://www.pinterest.com/mackbrownbooks/

Klout - http://klout.com/#/mackbrownbooks

Printed in Great Britain
by Amazon